Maximizing Your Memory Power

Second Edition
Danielle C. Lapp
Stanford University

BARRON'S

Dedication
To Jerry, who always makes it happen.

© Copyright 1998 by Barron's Educational Series, Inc.
Prior © Copyright 1992 by Barron's Educational Series, Inc.

All rights reserved.
No part of this book may be reproduced in any form, by
photostat, microfilm, xerography, or any other means, or
incorporated into any information retrieval system, electronic
or mechanical, without the written permission of the
copyright owner.

All inquiries should be addressed to:
Barron's Educational Series, Inc.
250 Wireless Boulevard
Hauppauge, New York 11788
http://www.barronseduc.com

Library of Congress Catalog Card No. 98-16506

International Standard Book No. 0-7641-0400-4

Library of Congress Cataloging-In-Publication Data

Lapp, Danielle C.
    Maximizing your memory power / Danielle C. Lapp. — 2nd ed.
        p.   cm. — (Barron's business success series)
    Includes bibliographical references and index.
    ISBN 0-7641-0400-4
    1. Mnemonics.   2. Success in business.   I. Title.   II. Series.
BF385.L26   1998
153.1'2—dc21   98-16506
                                                              CIP

PRINTED IN UNITED STATES OF AMERICA
98765432

Contents

Introduction

◆

This is a practical book on memory training applied to the business workplace. It explains how you can make the most of your memory once you understand how it functions, what hinders it, and what helps it. Although unconscious processes are at work, which is partly why people seldom can articulate what it is they do to remember, and even less what it is they fail to do when they forget, it is conscious strategies that will give you the satisfaction of remembering what you set out to remember. The news flash is, strategies can be taught and learned at any age. As to forgetting, prevention is the only cure.

To show the multiple applications of the principles governing good memory function, I have chosen specific examples referring to types of occupation rather than individuals. This should aid generalization, and encourage you to try the strategies outlined in this book. By learning to participate in the process, you will feel in control rather than out of control. You just need to start in small ways. The results are spectacular, and go beyond ego satisfaction; they show in your work and spill over into your private life, making you appear as a more thoughtful person.

In Part I, "Awareness," you will understand the mechanics of the memory process, and what you can do to help it. Important questions will be raised about what you expect to remember and your motivation for remembering. You will be urged to define goals, which proves essential for memory as well as good management on a small or larger scale. You will discover that most people do not tap a major resource, the senses, too often underused after childhood. You will learn about the stumbling blocks that interfere with memory function, and how to deal with them. Your new knowledge of memory and aging will allow you to cope better with the changes middle age brings.

In Part II, "Attention Management," you will focus on what pays off when you want to record a high quality memory trace: Selective Attention, Visualization, and Verbalization. In Part III, "Organization Management," you will learn to store information for easy recall by planting cues with the help of mnemonic systems. The principle of association, and more specifically image-association, underlies most mnemonics so useful to memorize names and faces, numbers, and lists. It can be extended to all kinds of information, as you will discover in other chapters. The key is to do *these mental operations in a conscious and systematic way*, using everything you have at your disposal—your emotions, your senses, and your intellect. That's the stuff memories are made of! Finally, the last chapter leads to a reflection on the role of memory in business management, closing the loop from personal goal setting to a more general planning, taking into account the knowledge of past experience.

There are no shortcuts to memory training, especially as one gets older. For maximum efficacy and generalization of the principles of good retention, the mnemonic training in Part III should come only after the basic training in "Awareness" and "Attention Management." Do not succumb, therefore, to the temptation of gobbling the tricks first. Begin reading Part I and Part II, then take your pick of the goodies according to your needs and interests. You will find them much more enjoyable as dessert. Good luck to you.

ACKNOWLEDGMENTS

I am extremely grateful to those who helped me with their insights, criticism, and encouragement. In particular, I would like to thank Professor Jerome Yesavage from Stanford University Medical School and Professor Guy Beauguillon from The Business School at the University of Nice, who read the manuscript. My editor, Linda Turner, and the illustrator, Deborah Zemke, deserve much of the credit for the finished product. "Gratitude is the heart's memory."

Part I

Awareness

Chapter 1

The Role Memory Plays in Life:

How Important Memory Really Is

Life is all memory, except for the one present moment that goes by you so quick you hardly catch it going.

—Tennessee Williams

AWARENESS FIRST!

Memory pervades our lives, because we live in a world punctuated by time. Without memory one would go through an everlasting present reduced to the second that swiftly vanishes into the past, and often into oblivion. Without memory, personality and experience would not exist and learning would be impossible. Memory gives continuity and meaning to our thoughts and actions by putting them into perspective. We use it all the time through thinking, comparing, evaluating, choosing, decision making, and imagining. All these mental operations rely on the brain's ability to store valuable information and refer to it.

Most people are unaware of the role memory plays in their lives because, like health, they take it for granted until it breaks down. Only when it does not work to their satisfaction, do they look into the mechanics of the memory process. Better late than never! One should not need to repair the damage, however; one could easily prevent it, if the right knowledge was acquired in school and the workplace. The lucky few who learn about memory training in their search for self improvement and job promotion discover, as you will, that they are only helpless if they believe in the miracle of passive memory. In fact, they can and must actively participate in the recording of memories in order to leave clear memory traces, by developing their sensory awareness, their sensitivity, and their observation skills. With new insights and mental strategies, they come to realize their mind could be a Ferrari rather than a Ford. Several research studies point out that, in general, people use only 10 percent of their mind capacity. The challenge is here for you to improve your memory with the guidance of a program proven successful to thousands of adults who have participated in our research studies at Stanford University.

Memory training both prevents and corrects forgetfulness at any age. It is like money in the bank.

WHAT IS A "GOOD ENOUGH" MEMORY?

Have you heard of the concept of a "good enough" parent, son, or daughter? This concept addresses the guilt people feel about not being perfect, that is, of just being human. It also occurs in the context of memory, and can be the cause of distress if we hope for the perfect memory that does not exist. Even extraordinary memories have their flaws; most are highly specialized and excel only in remembering specific information like numbers. Fortunately, provided we remember what we think we need to remember, most of us do not complain. But this is a subjective evaluation which, although satisfactory to us, does not tell the whole truth. Others may see flaws in our choice of what we remember, that is, our selective attention, especially in the workplace where objective criteria of memory performance are clearly defined. The first step should be to find out what these criteria are, and work towards remembering important information in particular.

If an ideal memory is a dream out of reach, a much better memory is a realistic goal. It can be improved beyond belief, as we learn what people with excellent memories do, and then do these things ourselves, applying their techniques voluntarily to our areas of expertise. It is that simple. In the daily battle against forgetting, let us use the whole battery of weapons, from simple visual reminders, to preventive organization and mnemonic systems.

But understanding is not enough: only practicing the principles of good retention improves memory.

HOW WOULD YOU RATE YOUR MEMORY?

Self-rating without tests is often inaccurate because it is subjective and highly emotional. Once you distrust your memory, you tend to notice only its failures. The older you get, the more you are inclined to worry about minor slips that happened before (as they do in normal memory function). The most common example is going into a room and suddenly wondering what you went there for. Back to where you started, a visual reminder cues you: you were reading, and you needed your notebook. Everyone has had this experience. At 20 we don't give it a second thought and identify the problem correctly: we got distracted. At 40 we start noticing the incidence of such episodes, asking "Am I slipping into middle age?" At 60 we wave the red flag of fear, wondering "Is this a prelude to Alzheimer's disease?" The judgment we make follows the curve of our anxiety, which, incidentally, is the number one cause of memory problems at any age. While you complain about your sudden decline, you may be surprised to hear your children say, "Dad, this is not new! You never remembered people's names, even my best friends'."

To restore a balance you must ask objective questions and find out which kind of information you remember well and which you have difficulties with. Try to pinpoint your weaknesses and your strengths, taking into account your assumptions. For instance, I used to say that I had a good memory for people, facts, art, languages, and literature, but a poor one for history and numbers because, I rationalized, I am not mathematically inclined and I care little about dates. Were there any numbers I was interested in, and therefore remembered well? Yes, prices! Prices are meaningful numbers to me, as I consider myself a good shopper eager to beat the system. This led me to revise all broad generalizations about what I can and cannot do. Moreover it gave me the incentive to try memory systems to challenge other numbers. They work without the motivation. One success leads to the next, and self-confidence ensues.

Here are the most common complaints. Are they yours? If you wish, check with friends and colleagues for another opinion on your forgetfulness. You may come to the realization that most people experience the same problems, which proves to be reassuring only to the extent that something can definitely be done about it.

My memory in general
Names and faces
Appointments

Where I put things

Words

Readings

What I was doing or saying before an interruption

What people tell me; messages

Places I have been

Directions and instructions

If you have any other difficulties, add them to this list. You will probably find your answers in one of the following chapters. But first, consider a basic and important question.

WHAT IS YOUR MOTIVATION FOR REMEMBERING?

If you have no motivation, you will not spontaneously make the effort to remember. Benjamin Franklin noticed humorously that "creditors have better memories than debtors." We all need a reason to act, and when the carrot is there, we act spontaneously because we get something out of it. At some stages in our lives, however, priorities change, modifying our motivation. If we do not realize it, we are likely to blame our memory, as did a 39-year-old psychologist I met at a conference. "I used to remember all the references I read once, but not anymore!" he pined. As I inquired about his possible lack of motivation, he had to admit that now he does not need to impress anyone, having reached his professional goal as head of his department. His memory had adjusted better than his ego to his life changes. The suggestion that he would soon find new ways to challenge his memory seemed to be somewhat reassuring.

Motivation is coated with emotion, the sweetener that makes us crave action. It is based on the belief in rewards or gratifications, as B. F. Skinner pointed out in his "Theory of Positive Reinforcement." A compliment promotes more positive change than a punishment. If you reward employees for remembering specific things, they will tend to remember things more often. If you reward initiative to remember miscellaneous things, you make people responsible for choosing their priorities. You can increase the odds of efficiency, however, by making it easier for people to remember. When objectives are few and clear, more people will respond to them, note Peters and Waterman in their best-seller *In Search of Excellence*. It is up to management to keep goals simple: "The excellent companies focus on only a few key business values, and a few objectives. This lets everyone know what is important, so there is simply less need for daily instructions (i.e., no daily short-term memory overload.)"

A smart way of defining objectives is *finding out what is most important to remember in your field*. Keep it short and simple. With this goal you will notice an increase in efficiency and success. Setting priorities helps memory by focusing and clearing the way. It will force you to analyze and evaluate your tasks. When I asked many business people what their priorities were, I realized most people could not tell me anything precise. You, too, may not be able to define priorities right away. But trying to do it will pay off. Here is a list of general priorities common to many businesses. You may wish to add your own:

- ◆ Commitments
- ◆ Knowing where to access information, sources (people, files, reference books)
- ◆ Paying bills before due date (to avoid penalties)
- ◆ Keeping in mind deadlines (to avoid last minute, rush-causing mistakes)

- Keeping track of important phone calls and meetings
- Mailing correspondence
- Answering letters
- Returning phone calls
- Remembering the people you deal with (The more detailed the information the better: file name, company rank, relation to your business, personal data, impression.)
- Numbers, tables, and figures (to compare and quote when needed)
- Facts
- Contributions
- Articles and reviews
- Reports
- Books on a subject
- Quotations and references
- Handling several important projects at the same time
- Dealing with several people with conflicting interests or points of view

In his interesting book, *The Seven Habits of Highly Effective People*, Stephen Covey points out that "No involvement, no commitment"; the key to motivation is getting yourself and others involved. His maxim for personal effectiveness is "Manage from the left brain (logical, analytical), but lead from the right (intuitive, creative, visual)." Keeping both present in mind at any time is the key to success and a successful memory. Once motivated, make and keep commitments. Be responsible and do what has to be done, even if you dislike it. The successful person has the habit of doing what the failures don't like to do. Like T. J. Watson, founder of IBM, put it: "Success is on the far side of failure." Above all, success requires acting upon decisions, and following through until they are implemented. This also helps memory.

HOW IMPORTANT IS MEMORY IN THE WORKPLACE?

Memory is the key to efficiency and good management of any given task. Imagine what it would be like if everybody forgot what had been learned, the rules to work by, time and place, assignments, deadlines, what people said, and promises made. Fortunately, catastrophic situations like forgetting to put the screws on the tail of a passenger plane during maintenance seldom happen. Many small types of forgetfulness, however, may erode a business or a partnership, and compromise a career. People who are attentive to what is important to remember on the job have the edge. They may rise faster along the corporate ladder and make the enterprise more successful.

Examples of forgetfulness abound, and one may wonder how businesses survive in spite of them. A travel agent recalls the time she forgot to get visas for her customers, who were then turned away at the foreign airport . . . or the time chaos ensued when she confused the date on a client's schedule by skipping a day. Another time a colleague failed to check the new time schedule, and the customer missed his plane. The consequences of such forgetfulness by one or several employees may create all kinds of hassle, from losing customers to lawsuits. With cost effectiveness in mind, the manager's option may not be as simple as firing the absent-minded but trained employee. Requiring selective attention training for all employees could prevent this from ever happening. As the saying goes: "An ounce of prevention is worth a pound of cure."

Attention management and organizational strategies can easily be learned and practiced.

In business, I found out that the important information revolves about people, relationships between them, and technical information relating to the task at hand. Intelligent organization and memory go hand in hand.

HOW TO CAPITALIZE ON YOUR MEMORY

You capitalize on your memory by training it in the areas you need most. *Learning* capacity has a direct effect on *earning* capacity because, as the famous psychologist William James put it, "The man whose acquisitions stick, is the man who is always achieving and advancing, whilst his neighbors, spending most of their time in relearning what they once knew but have forgotten, simply hold their own."

In an article about job strategies, journalist Jane Elizabeth Allen wrote that businesses and individuals who remain successful share four characteristics related to memory:

1. *Know what they do well.* Ms. Allen calls such skills "core competencies," and they include people competencies, mechanical competencies, computer competencies, and visual and verbal competencies. The advantage goes to those who know their "core competencies" and stick with them. (Practicing keeps them in memory.)

2. *Do it fast!* She argues that success in today's volatile world is based not only on what you know but even more on using what you know quickly. The advantage goes to those who respond both quickly and correctly. ("Do it now, when you think of it" is a very effective memory management strategy.)

3. *Improve it constantly.* The continuous improvement process is called "kaizen" in Japanese and gives the advantage to those who keep improving. (Keeping your mind on it keeps it alive in your memory.)

4. *Collaborate with others, including competitors.* The competitively successful see everybody as a potential ally or potential resource. The advantage does not go to those who know the important people, but to those who treat every person as important. (Remember people and what makes them tick.)

In sum, to survive in the corporate jungle, *know your stuff, do it well, improve, and collaborate.* In other words, *use your memory widely and wisely.*

While developing habits that lead to top quality recording, storage, and recall of what you need to remember, you will increase both your memory and your efficiency. Instead of passively waiting for things to come back, you will make them come back using simple strategies. The art of memory lies in action: Do the right thing to remember, and you will, because you will have planted a cue. Recall is the most difficult part of the process. It is facilitated by *a system of cues placed at the time of recording.* Training your memory to suit your purpose is your best insurance policy against forgetting. It will prevent cluttering your mind with things you ought to forget—at least temporarily! It is all a matter of organization and practice of skills.

COMPUTER FRIENDLY?

In this age of automation, it is possible to prevent catastrophic lapses by relying on your friend the computer to remind you of due dates for such things as filing taxes, mailing grants, or picking up a client at the airport. If it has the capability, set it up regularly. It is also the best and most complex filing system you can imagine. Use all its possibilities to organize as best you can. Make diagrams, mini posters, striking memos to help others remember. Mechanical reminders should be used sparingly, however, and for important matters only. Keep in mind that you may not always have access to a computer, or there may be a shortage of electricity.

The other downside of relying too heavily on technology is that people may stop assuming responsibility and making the effort to train their memory. It has been said that since children have been given calculators, fewer bother to learn the multiplication tables. It is better to get into the habit of relying on mental strategies to do simple calculations and to remember things to do, errands to run, and topics to deal with. It keeps your mind sharp and prevents your memory from slipping into disuse. Using both mental and mechanical aids is the best insurance policy.

UNDERSTANDING YOUR GOALS

All literature on success emphasizes the fact that success happens only if goals are clearly defined. Once this is done, it is relatively easy to determine a strategy on which to focus energy and resources. Too often goals get forgotten along the line, and this is one of the main reasons for failure. As it is impossible to row in a straight line without keeping one's eyes on a fixed point, it is impossible to reach a goal without focusing on it and having it always present in mind. Mr. Honda's success is credited to his long-range goals of consistent quality in small- and mid-size cars with fuel economy performance. His Honda Civic, which gets 51 miles per gallon and is able to go 65 mph uphill, is the proof that power and reduced gas consumption can be realized at a reasonable price, which Detroit denied being possible. His main goal was always to give the consumer what he or she wanted, and he found a way to do it: he designed a more aerodynamic body with lighter parts, and set out to build the prototype, while others seemed to reject the idea and did not research the possibilities.

On a smaller scale, it may help to define simple goals and achieve high efficiency in stressful situations. For instance, a hospital secretary in her late fifties complained that she had difficulty dealing with the numerous phone calls. She would pick up the phone, and by the time she dialed the number of the phone correspondent she had forgotten the name of the calling party. She needed a strategy to unburden her. I suggested she keep a spiral notebook with the daily date, and that she write the names of all the callers as they announce themselves. Not only did she solve her problem, but she noticed she even had an edge on her younger colleagues since she was keeping track of all the calls listed in order, including their phone numbers in case it proved necessary to call back. Such strategies compensate for the effects of aging, like the difficulty of doing several things at the same time. It also makes the difference between good and excellent, at any age.

STATING WHAT NEEDS TO BE REMEMBERED

The Product or the Task: A Clear Definition

What is most important to remember in a job situation is not always obvious to the employee. The initial training should highlight the main tasks so that attention can be focused on those tasks. The negative consequences of not attending to them should also be emphasized to add an emotional impact to the information. The expectations of the employer should also be mentioned. For example, Josephine Wong, an executive at Merrill Lynch, told me the most important flaw she saw in her assistants was "not following through with a task until it is completed. They will do something partially, passing it along to someone else, and forget about it, until it comes back to haunt them." They wait for the client to call back instead of returning his call, or they think that by entering a request for information in the computer it will be forwarded. Since we work in a complex web of machines monitored by people, we must assume that they may not react to the demand as eagerly as we do, partly because their motivation may be weaker than ours, and partly because of the hectic pace of demands put on everyone.

The only way to guarantee that things are done is to check the different steps, making sure others are doing their part. A client who is ready to invest wants the information *now*. There is nothing more frustrating than having to wait to give it to him, especially when all the technology is there to help. But it is people who make it work. Ms. Wong confirmed the fact that the way to a promotion is efficacy. "Get things done, and you will get there, especially since there are so few people who do it right!" Moreover, by completing the tasks methodically you will not burden your memory, dispatching most of the work in the right order and time.

Good habits of attending immediately to the most urgent tasks require organization: *set priorities and do not procrastinate*. Once you have established a reputation for reliability and thoroughness you will have it made with bosses as well as clients, and success will ensue. If motivation is the driving force, organization is the key that unlocks all possibilities. Use every trick in the book. Tools to trigger recall are numerous.

Auditory reminders, like a timer, alarm clock, or watch will help you keep time for things to do, while freeing you to concentrate on something else in the meantime. It could be as simple an example as having to call somebody at a certain time, or finishing something before the mail goes out.

Visual reminders are a must. Keep the files to complete and the reports to send out on top of an uncluttered desk and pause now and then to acknowledge what you have there. (Otherwise they may become part of the decor and you will not notice them anymore. Familiarity dulls attention.) Also write down priorities on a "daily things to do" pad. Order helps memory while lack of order clutters it. You may also make some diagrams using your visual memory to remember important points, reviewing them often until they are engraved in your mind. This is especially useful for tasks you need to repeat frequently.

People

People are important in business at every step of the operation, from janitors and couriers to secretaries, managers, and executives. A lot has to be done by many people before completing a deal. Also, deals are done or undone by them. In sales for instance, it pays to make it a point to remember personal information about people in addition to their business status and what it is they want from you. One must know their name, personal background, likes and dislikes, weaknesses and strengths.

Practical information should be written down for further reference on a file: phone number, purpose in relation to you, date and place

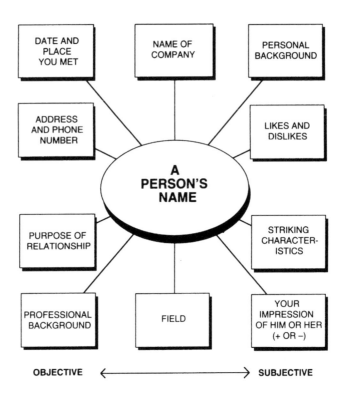

Figure 1
Information to Remember About People

(Suggestion: Make your own diagrams to remember information about a product, a company, an organization, a process, a procedure, and so on.)

you met, and initial impression, as featured in Figure 1. Several sections in the book mention people in different contexts. You will see how you can identify all their important characteristics, form a good image of each, and finally link them together in a useful retrieval system. These mental strategies applied to people should be considered a model for identifying and linking information on any complex topic.

Notice that there are objective and subjective elements to remember. These elements all contribute to a good working relationship. People sign the deal with the most able person who often seems more "on the ball" than the next competitor. As Mel Brooks put it in an interview: "I rehearse important facts a little and remember significant details to help me make the deal." Your homework should be reviewing the relevant information and listing the characteristics of the things attached to the deal.

In addition to the rational aspect of the interaction there is the emotional one: People buy from a salesman they find sympathetic because he addresses their needs or objections. I remember not buying a car because the salesman was sloppy in manner and appearance. Munching on his lunch as we talked, this man did not seem interested in selling. I just went to another dealer who was. I also remember buying three kimonos from a lovely little old lady in Tokyo just because she was so gracious showing them all and trying to find the one that looked prettiest on me. Subtle but honest flattery is often part of the strategy, and we all know it pays off. Who does not like feeling appreciated, even knowing there is self-interest behind the compliment?

It has been said that President Lyndon Johnson got most of his bills passed by establishing good relationships with the senators and representatives. He was a master at making deals, in part because he remembered what each of them wanted and what made them tick.

The way to record specific information and have it available to you when you need it is explained throughout the following chapters.

There are principles of attention management and mnemonic systems to remember names, numbers, and lists. However, your willingness to dwell on important points, that is, likes or dislikes, may be enough to strongly associate the person to the situation because emotion is a strong component of memory. You will then remember the information when you think of him or her.

Using visualization in combination with a verbal comment is most effective, as our research studies have shown. When meeting someone, therefore, make a comment about the place, time of year, and circumstances. You will soon get used to an inner monologue with pictures in the background: by directing your own movie-making, you will remember more.

BECOMING AWARE OF WHAT YOU FEAR TO FORGET

It is often easier to say what we do *not* like than what we like, perhaps because of the unpleasantness of it. Likewise, it is simpler to state what we fear to forget in a given situation than trying to say what we should remember. Here the fear to forget proves to be an advantage, since by anticipating your forgetfulness you will prevent it most of the time. Preventive strategies come in two forms: immediate action or delayed action, planting a cue for later recall.

If you know you may forget to sign a report because you are not happy with it:

◆ *Do it now when you think of it*, and get it out of the way.

If you dread bringing home a project that must be in by tomorrow:

◆ *Put it in your briefcase* when the idea occurs to you.

Planning is organizing. Spend some time thinking and commenting on what you should not forget, and make an association with something you are going to see or do. For instance, return keys to the desk before leaving.

Visualize:

The keys

The desk

Your purse. All together.

Upon seeing your purse, you will see the keys and the desk.

This is a simple application of the principle of image-association basic to so many memory strategies. You can get into the habit of dwelling on what you fear to forget. By blowing up the imagined incident you are recording it better, especially if you associate it with an object you are bound to see.

People usually have painful memories of incidents of forgetfulness with tragic consequences such as missed commitments, appointments, meetings, or deadlines. By paying special attention to them you can prevent the repeat performance. Plant strong reminders you cannot miss, but mainly *pause* and *think often about the important event.*

For general things to do, simply review your daily schedule on your appointment calendar, taking a few seconds to think about each event, visualizing and commenting on it, associating it with something else happening the same day, and chances are you will not forget. Get into the habit of consulting your calendar several times per day, first thing in the morning, at noon, and in the late afternoon. Also look each day at your whole week to put things you have to do in a broader perspective. In addition, it will help you remember your commitments when scheduling a new event on the spur of the moment. For people who travel, a regular glance at the trips you need to take within a month's period may make it easier to schedule social gatherings with friends and relatives. In business it is efficient to write the phone numbers and references of strangers one is to call or meet.

The more events you have to deal with, the more you must organize. You will help your memory by writing down, in a personal pocket date book, relevant information you may want to access at any time. You will thus keep your mental energy to record information relating to your topic. The older one gets, the more important this proves to be, because it becomes increasingly difficult to handle several tasks simultaneously.

Using memory systems you will learn in Part III will help recall of many items, including numbers, ideas, topics, and things to do. Being foolproof, they will release your anxiety. The use of stickers on the steering wheel of the car is an emergency option for the more distracted among us. Use it sparingly! In general, I prefer to use my brain; at least it does not fall off. But any trick is good provided it works for you. Give it a try and come up with your own examples.

Anticipate what you may forget and organize accordingly, *planting cues* to help recall. *Review frequently* what you want to keep fresh in mind, every time making a *comment to reinforce* the memory trace.

THE EMOTIONAL FACTOR

Memories get distorted by the emotional factor. For example, at the time I was asked to rate the car dealer where I bought my car, I noticed that a small bad experience seemed to overshadow all the other good ones, tilting my judgment negatively. In order to be fair, I had to put it into perspective and finally dismiss it as unimportant: the salesman had shown signs of impatience on a single occasion, when I pointed out my displeasure that no one was there in the service department at the time I had made an appointment to have something corrected. Bad memories, like bad impressions, stick longer than others because they are upsetting, and monopolize strong emotions. The more we dwell on them, the more we reinforce them. Beware and be aware!

PERSONALITY

Our likes or dislikes, our beliefs and prejudices determine much of our Selective Attention when we are on automatic pilot, that is, when we are unaware of our selection. Our personality predisposes us to accept or reject whatever comes our way, which among other things, affects learning. Studies on older adults show that *self-esteem, an openness to new ideas and experiences, and a vivid imagination facilitate new learning;* whereas, rigidity, stubbornness, impatience, lack of self-discipline, or poor self-esteem lead to rejection of new strategies or abandonment of a program before it is given a chance to prove that it works. If people were willing to try new strategies, and not turn their backs on them, they would often succeed where they are sure to fail without that valuable information. I suggest they try with small things with no adverse consequences, and seeing that it works will encourage them to try with more important applications.

Although it is difficult and perhaps impossible to change personality, one can modify mental attitudes when one recognizes attitudes that are detrimental to one's goals. Just acknowledge that these attitudes are counterproductive and should be dealt with. For instance, you can learn to listen better, observe better, and pick up a few pointers to remember specific information you value. I hear people say, "It will not work for me," before they even start the mnemonic training. They sabotage themselves through lack of self-confidence or self-esteem. I assume that by not carrying this baggage, you will give yourself a chance and apply the method! It is the only way to shed those fears and negative expectations when they exist. Try it, you'll like it!

PRINCIPLE 1

State clearly what needs to be remembered.

Chapter 2

◆

Understanding Memory Function:

Different Aspects of Memory at Work

Memory is the thing you forget with.

—Alexander Chase

HOW MEMORY WORKS: THE CHAIN

Think of memory as a chain made of these essential links:

Need or Interest → Motivation → Attention →
Concentration → Organization

Need or *interest* gives the *motivation* to pay *attention* and to transform it into *concentration*, using *organization*. When basic needs or interests disappear people become dysfunctional, which happens if they are overly anxious, preoccupied, or depressed. Only by removing anxiety and obsessive and depressive thoughts can one restore spontaneous motivation. The degree of motivation determines how long attention is sustained. Depending on how efficiently one concentrates and organizes, one leaves a better or poorer memory trace. Memory training can help improve the last three links of the chain. The first two depend on personality and the circumstances of one's life. By becoming aware of the process, one can redirect motivation and even discover objective needs. This is the case after major changes in life, like leaving school, changing jobs or relocating, divorce, widowhood, or retirement. They all lead to disruptions affecting motivation, attention, and concentration.

Whenever any of these links are broken, memory cannot operate and a deficit appears. Anxiety and depressive thoughts are the major causes of memory problems at any age because they hit at the root. In these states, the first three links are missing and concentration cannot be sustained. Thinking is short-circuited; therefore the organization needed to record and store information is reduced. The mind is only preoccupied with worries and obsessive thoughts. People with a lot on their minds are not free to think properly.

VOLUNTARY VERSUS INVOLUNTARY MEMORY

Involuntary memory is given to us on a silver platter through the miracle of the senses. It is an easy type of memory based on recognition. Sensory awareness triggers recall of a similar past experience. A smell of apple pie wafting along down the street suddenly transports you back to your childhood—it was the smell that welcomed you every time you visited your grandmother. If you are receptive to the stream of associations, you will soon recapture many other details of the times you spent there.

People seldom allow their senses and their imagination to retrieve memories. They seem too much in a hurry to attend to the present. Those who, like the French author Marcel Proust, are sensitive enough to dwell on their sensations, have access to a wealth of past images and feelings. From the taste of a cookie dipped in tea, Proust managed to bring back to life the special moments of his childhood holidays at his aunt's, and he marvels: "Combray and its surroundings, everything taking shape and volume sprung out, city and gardens, from my cup of tea."

Voluntary memory, however, is not a chance encounter but a conscious operation. It is what we do to prompt recall of something we want to remember. It involves an active and inquisitive mind. It is the part we can control, although even involuntary memory can be provoked by observation and sensory awareness training. We use both all the time but not as effectively as we could. Otherwise, we would not experience most memory slips. Fortunately, once we learn memory devices, we can rely more on them than on the mere coincidence of involuntary memory. The latter is a free gift we cannot count on, whereas the former is a sure thing, provided we make it a point to remember and act accordingly. We can make the most of both, as we learn more about memory.

SHORT-TERM VERSUS LONG-TERM MEMORY

Short- and long-term memory are two different types of memory responding to the need of remembering information for a longer or shorter time. It is a very efficient system meant to free the mind from irrelevant information. (See Figure 2.)

Short-term memory deals with material meant to be used immediately or within 30 seconds. It allows the brain to dispatch information as soon as it has been used, thus directing attention to the next

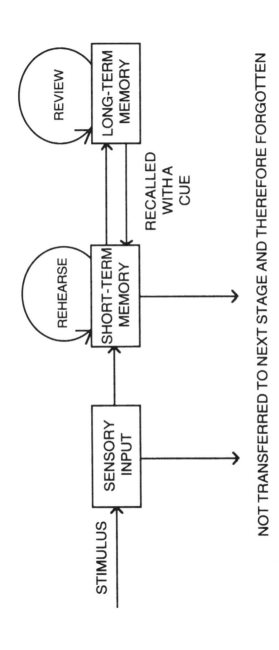

Figure 2
Short-term and Long-term Memory

item as is the case in typing, reading, or taking notes. As soon as this item is acted upon, it disappears; but if we fail to act, as is the case during an interruption dialing a phone number, the number vanishes and we have to look it up again. Short-term memory is extremely fragile because there is no time to leave a trace. It can only be sustained through action or repetition. This type of memory has the function of clearing the mind of used information, an automatic eraser that prevents overcrowding, while screening for the present needs only. It is also referred to as "working memory" because it acts as a scratch pad on which one can temporarily retain as many as seven items of information (such as telephone numbers). If the information is not used immediately it is forgotten or transferred into long-term memory.

Long-term memory is a more complex mental operation that entails *depth of processing* resulting in a memory trace. That is, the information is recorded and given time to be stored for further recall. This operation is done through a complex web of factors, emotional and analytical, referred to in the jargon as "encoding." Depending on how efficient the encoding and storage, recall will be aided or hindered, which explains why some memories stick better than others, and why some people have better memories than their peers. Everyone can help in the process, actively participating rather than passively expecting miracles that do not usually happen. When we remember, it is not a miracle—*we do something*, and when we forget, we do not. It is that simple.

MEMORY CAPACITY

Precisely because of this dual system, there is no need to worry about running out of memory capacity, especially since even long-term memories can be temporarily erased or pushed back into the subconscious.

As the brain ages, it may seem more crowded, and the filing system less accurate for newer information, partly because the brain's metabolism slows down, and new recordings are not as clear. Research has isolated a lack of spontaneous organization in older subjects, hinting that they do not generate strategies and consequently may have more difficulty sorting out and discarding what is not important to remember. The storage space, however, is adequate provided that space is not used for anxious ruminations and depressive thoughts, which take up the memory capacity and create a handicap in many people. Studies have proven that getting rid of anxiety and depression restores adequate capacity. Instead of worrying about the fear of forgetting or their inability to perform the task, subjects learn to use proven strategies that give them the confidence they need to facilitate recording and recall.

THE FUNCTION OF FORGETTING

The new cognitive theory challenges the belief that we forget *permanently* many things we learned. Rather than being erased, they are pushed aside because of disuse, and lack of relevance in the present. The memory trace exists somewhere but is hard to find. It is a retrieval failure, the problem being the accessibility of the information, not its existence. We know that it can be brought back to consciousness through involuntary memory cues, or voluntary organized cued recall. The pragmatic aspect of memory explains the role *forgetting* plays in the process, even to include the psychoanalytical theory of repression of painful material one cannot deal with.

First, as hinted above, forgetting prevents crowding of the active channels. Second, it allows us to sustain attention by temporarily freeing the mind to focus on one thing at a time. Third, it unburdens the present from the weight of the past, especially in regard to negative memories involving suffering. There are things we must forget if we are to get on with our lives. As Matthew Arnold put it "We forget because we must, not because we will." Sometimes, in the case of traumatic events, it may prove more difficult to forget than to remember, because of the constant rehashing of obsessional thoughts monopolizing the mind. Most people, however, manage to leave behind what cannot be undone without major neuroses! Let us heed this warning: It may prove wise in all walks of life to keep remembering the positive lessons learned from negative episodes. As William James said: "The art of being wise is the art of knowing what to overlook." At work and at home it means forgetting and forgiving minor flaws, for everyone's sake.

THE THREE STEPS: RECORDING, STORAGE, AND RECALL

Each step requires our full attention and participation, but we seldom oblige. To make a top quality recording we must use everything we have at our disposal: our senses, our mind, our sensibility, our feelings, and even our moods. Research has shown that efficient mental strategies take all of them into account. You will soon discover how.

Recording

Too often we think we have recorded something, but we haven't if our attention was not there. Not everything we encounter is recorded. We screen and choose, consciously or subconsciously. To gain control of recording, one must isolate attention deficits. Too often we blame our memory in a situation in which it could not operate, like when we are in a hurry, rushed, anxious, worried, emotionally upset, tired, under the influence of alcohol or drugs, when we are interrupted, and when we perform automatic gestures. If nothing is recorded, there is nothing to recall.

The only way to guarantee a good recording is to be aware of doing it *consciously*. Don't just file a report, tell yourself you are doing it, and take a mental picture of your hand on that particular file. Comment on the time and on the completion of the task. Record your emotional reaction—satisfaction, irritation—and if you can, anticipate what will come of it. Plant a cue for recall by making associations as you store the information. Later on, just thinking about it will bring back your actions and comments.

Storage

The filing system works by *categories* that range from general to personal, including emotions. We remember better what touches us, and we can exploit this fact by getting emotionally involved, and becoming aware of it, at the time of recording. Like a library, the storage system must have cross references so that we can get access to the information from several sources, intellectual as well as emotional.

For practical reasons memories are stored in relation to use. I chose the image of "the layer system" to explain why and how some memories are accessible at a given time, and others are not. Although all of them can be resuscitated haphazardly by involuntary memory, some are closer to consciousness than others. They are the things we need and use in daily life. The rest gets filed along the following lines:

CONSCIOUSNESS

ACTIVE	*Daily necessary information (easy recall)* *Used continuously*	*BLUE*
PASSIVE	*Information referred to less often* *Recognition memory excellent*	*RUST*
LATENT	*Much information stored since childhood* *Needs a cue to return to consciousness* *Stimulus-response involuntary memory*	*GRAY*

SUBCONSCIOUS

To remember the way memories are stored, use your imagination and visualize activity in the blue layer of the present (files in and out at all times), passivity in the rust layer of yesterday, and sleeping beauty in the gray layer of long ago.

Recall

Prompted recall is easy because a cue triggers recognition, the easiest type of memory. We have mentioned the miracle of involuntary memory where a cue is offered to us when we least expect it. It may trigger buried 30-year-old memories, like the name of a child in our kindergarten class. It is well known that multiple choice or true and false tests are easier than essay tests, and it is believed they don't accurately test memory because of the guessing effect. If we learn to plant cues at the time of recording, we prompt recall. Principles of good retention and mnemonic systems help you do it. The art of memory is the art of planting cues. Most people are familiar with a few: acronyms like UNESCO, CIA, or HOMES (to remember the great lakes of the United States). Here

you will learn many more systems of cues, and above all, the principles behind them.

USING BOTH SIDES OF THE BRAIN: THE RATIONAL AND THE EMOTIONAL

One of the most important ideas in *The Search of Excellence* is the acknowledgment that successful companies use both reason and intuition in their leadership, tapping both sides of the brain. The most common mistake in management seems to be unilateral confidence in analytical ability with a total disregard for the emotional. The gut feeling that often stems from experience is an unarticulated memory.

Using the Rational Side

In business everything seems to be approached from a rational point of view. Sales are numbers. There is supposedly a logic behind every task. The markets follow curves that can be explained logically if not predicted. Experts analyze all kinds of situations, except the emotional components that go with them. Of course, everyone knows that the stock market is sensitive to emotional public reaction, or the sneeze of the president, but the analysts like to underplay what cannot be controlled. Perhaps that is why people in general, and relationships with clients in particular, are given such a low priority in most companies. (Nordstrom department stores stand out as an exception, which accounts for their success.)

We sure want to believe that we make rational decisions, not taking our emotions into account, but do we really? Paradoxically, studies on cognitive biases by experimental psychologists Tversky and Kahneman show that we are more influenced by stories than by data. In a typical experiment, subjects are told about a man: his age and family situation, and the fact that he is conservative, careful, serious, and not interested in politics but in his hobbies of solving puzzles, sailing, and wood carving. Then these subjects learn that this description was taken from a sample of the population containing 80 percent lawyers and 20 percent engineers. When asked what this man's profession is likely to be the subjects pick their answer on the basis of the stereotype of the occupation rather than the statistical sample.

Thus even when we reason, we spontaneously tend to use emotional responses first, rather than rational ones. If conclusions often follow stereotypes rather than data, it is partly because they are more concrete and appeal to our feelings, whereas data is abstract and neutral. Subconsciously, the stereotypes have left a deeper memory trace than the numbers, hence they seem more familiar, more reliable as a source of experienced truth, and we tend to refer to them first.

With this information in mind, it follows that it is wise to review our decisions, asking why we think we made them. It may make us aware of our prejudices and stereotypes and thus allow us to keep them in check. It may also reveal the source of our "gut feelings," which may or may not prove to be accurate and valuable good instincts rooted in past experience.

Using the Emotional Side

Advertising is more aware than any other business of the way people react to publicity and to the labeling and packaging of products, and they capitalize on people's fears, their libido, and their aspirations, with subliminal seduction. This means we are not aware of what affects us and how. For instance, a simple label or packaging can attract or detract the buyer. Cleaning products sell in green and blue, but not in brown. Interior decorators are now decorating offices because it is a fact that light, color, shapes, and the degree of comfort of furniture may increase or decrease efficiency and create a mood that is more conducive to harmonious cooperation. The Japanese are even introducing music and fragrances released in the offices, because it relaxes the mind, reducing stress and making people happier while working.

Studies have shown that mood and emotion play an important part in consolidating the memory trace. If you were asked to remember specific work experiences right off the bat, chances are you will hit upon the best and the worst, the ones you considered successes or failures, the people with whom you were in sync, and the difficult employee. In other words you remember the episodes in which you got emotionally involved.

Establishing relations is essential to efficient business. The Japanese concern for the other person may partly account for Japan's economic success. It is a culture of people who believe that the welfare of the group comes first. Only then can they reap personal benefits. They are careful, therefore, not to antagonize anyone, and to conform to the rules set by their leaders. To do so, they must remember a great deal of personal information and be constantly aware of people's reactions. Perhaps the role of ritual in their lives can be seen as a constant reminder that unburdens their memory. For example, kinesthetic or movement memory makes it possible to remember without effort the various depths of the bows they take by greeting each other according to their hierarchical order. Since this is most important, failure to do so results in being ostracized.

MOOD AND MEMORY ARE RELATED

We tend to remember information in the same mood we have recorded it. This explains the stream of recollections of the same kind. When we are telling jokes, for instance, more come to mind; when we are sad, it seems only sad memories are stored in our minds. Moods do trigger memories as do the senses, and we could use that fact to remember more information on a subject we know we have registered in a certain mood (for instance, a phone conversation when sad and lonely away from home). For it does not require the skill of an actor to change one's mood. Music, light, reading, food, nature, art, pictures, and the evocation of memories can switch moods. The "matching of moods and environment" is quite amazing. An experiment has shown that one remembers better what has been learned in the water when one is in that element. If this were true, ideally one should take exams or be interviewed for a job in one's study!

We can also change our mood before a performance. Stage and movie artists, as well as competing athletes, have long trained in visualization and positive thinking to capitalize on their past victories. A successful businessman recalled how he pumped himself before what he anticipated to be a hard sale by thinking about his last successful sale and reviewing the arguments that made it happen. As he recaptured the positive mood, his confidence increased, and he went into the meeting in the right mood to make his pitch. It helped him win.

PRINCIPLE 2

Participate actively in the Recording, Storage, and Recall of information.

Chapter 3

The Stumbling Blocks:

*What Prevents Memory
from Operating Smoothly*

The highest possible stage in moral culture is when we recognize that we ought to control our thoughts.

—Charles Darwin

NEGATIVE MENTAL ATTITUDES: HOW THEY AFFECT MEMORY

We act according to our beliefs, and our mental attitudes determine our actions. If we believe we cannot rely on our memory, we do not even try. By giving up, we let it dwindle, for it needs practice to remain activated. *Hopelessness, helplessness, and worthlessness are the negative attitudes* preventing acting on memory problems. If you think you are too old to learn new material, or are not good at numbers, names, or data, you feel hopeless and worthless and you cannot help yourself. This is where "pulling yourself up by your own bootstraps" does not seem to work because you have not identified the problem. As soon as you have, you can modify your negative attitude with the knowledge that certain strategies can help your memory at any age. Just be willing to try them and see the results. Only your success will help you change your mental attitudes.

The method you are learning here will convince you that the mind needs directions and that it is up to you to learn them and follow them. Your memory will react well to these new instructions, and you will remember what you set out to remember, shedding negative expectations in the process.

A common work-related negative attitude especially hard to dislodge is *perfectionism*. He who says "I should do better" is always dissatisfied because his ideal is perfection, an unreachable, undefined goal. As the motivational speaker Les Brown says to debunk perfectionists: "Practice makes better, not perfect." Although one can always get better, one will never get perfect since perfection does not exist in reality. Thus, stop saying, "I should remember everything I forget," and try working on your memory a step at a time.

RELIEVING ANXIETY THROUGH RELAXATION

Thinking and memory require a state of relaxed alertness. Perhaps that is why so many great ideas have sprung while taking a walk or swimming, rather than in front of a desk. There are simple steps to reduce anxiety, starting with physical relaxation and moving towards mental relaxation through visualization exercises. Any time we are put on the spot to perform, a flurry of anxiety lurks in the background. An easy deep breathing exercise can restore mind control by keeping thoughts away from the anxiety and onto the task.

The Waves

Breathe deeply and gradually through the nose, visualizing a wave building up as you inhale, and roll back and dissolve gradually on the shore as you exhale, to be reborn again in a new wave. Always start by exhaling to empty your lungs for maximum capacity. Then inhale slowly, gradually, visualizing the wave until it reaches its crest at the top of filling your lungs. Exhale slowly, following the wave on its journey back to the shore where it dissolves. The exhalation is twice as long as the inhalation, and the rhythm should be smooth and regular, in harmony with the image of a gentle summer wave. Do it several times in a row, without forcing. Enjoy!

Progressive Muscle Relaxation Combined with Visualization

This technique is an excellent mental hygiene exercise that I recommend and practice before going to bed because it is so relaxing that it induces sleepiness. (Incidentally, it has proven effective for people with insomnia who were told to do it whenever they woke up during the night.) It makes you more aware of the tension you had built up, and allows you to discard it for a better night's rest. This carries over into your day, making you more relaxed, open and available, and therefore more efficient. It also improves your mood since you feel less hassled and more in control of your stress. The result is a more confident and pleasant person to work with. Try it tonight, before you go to bed.

Visualize a place you associate with beauty, calm, and harmony—a lake shore, for instance. Imagine you are lying there in a perfect setting focusing on the lake.

You are going to tense one set of muscles at a time for 10 seconds and release them suddenly, watching the effects of relaxation on the muscles—a certain warmth and tingling—before starting on a new set of muscles.

Lie down on your bed and first bend your knees in order to work on the lower part of the leg.

1. Point your toes away from you, lifting your heels, and tense up for 10 seconds. Relax suddenly, focusing on the physical sensation the relaxation produces on the front part of the lower leg.

2. Point your toes towards you, digging your heels, and tense up for 10 seconds. Relax, focusing on the sensation.

   Now, with extended legs, repeat #1 and #2.

3. Next, lift your arms, making a fist of each hand and tense up for 10 seconds, stretching forward until you feel your back muscles without straining. Now drop your arms and enjoy the feeling of relaxation.

4. Lift your arms again, this time making a star with your stretched out hands, fingertips wide apart. Tense up for 10 seconds, stretching forward, then drop your arms and enjoy the feeling of relaxation. (In addition, these arm exercises also relax the shoulders and the lower neck muscles.)

5. Tense the muscles of your face by stretching your open mouth forward forming an O. Hold 10 seconds, and release. (This, by the way, will bring color to your cheeks. You can do it independently anytime, anywhere.)

Now, check the relaxation of your muscles by giving them a direct order to relax individually. While visualizing them, say slowly to yourself in a monotone:

Relax your feet, relax your toes, relax your ankles, relax your legs, relax your knees, relax your thighs, relax your tummy, relax your stomach, relax your chest, relax your shoulders, relax your upper arms, relax your forearms, relax your wrists, relax your hands, relax your fingers, relax your neck, relax your face, relax your jaw, relax your mouth, relax your tongue, relax your lips, relax your cheeks, relax your nose, relax your eyes, relax your eyelids, relax your eyebrows, relax your forehead, relax your scalp, relax your ears.

Now focus on your soothing image of the lake, and enjoy your relaxation. Chances are you will fall asleep at this point. Notice that I have extensively detailed the muscles in the visualization part of the exercise, because more time is needed for inducing the state of profound relaxation that brings about sleep or the state called self-hypnosis.

Once you see the benefits of these simple exercises you will do them every day to keep stress under control. It will serve your memory by making you more aware, more attentive, and more selective for

better concentration. Do "the waves" anywhere, anytime you feel a pang of anxiety. It will nip it in the bud!

ANXIETY REDUCTION

Anxiety reduction exercises are very helpful to put you in the optimum condition for excellent performance, whenever adrenaline is bound to flow. Whether it is before closing a deal, giving a lecture or a talk, making a presentation, firing or hiring employees, giving an ultimatum or negotiating a contract, anticipation and visualization will help you focus on the issues and the way to bring them forward effectively.

Anticipation

Anticipation forces you to review your material and your arguments, and gives you time to evaluate them and revise them if necessary. It also helps you memorize them through review and analysis which include personal emotional considerations. You will pinpoint the difficult aspects and deal with them with special care. (This is selective attention at work.) From anticipating your own and other people's reactions, you will deal better with the situation. Putting yourself in the others' shoes does more than help in the transaction through emotional empathy which you must be sure to communicate; it also gives you leverage by allowing you to think of all the possible scenarios. Have an answer to all the hypothetical questions and you will feel relaxed, dropping the anxiety stemming from the unknown. This self-questioning will prevent the effects of overconfidence, as happened to a retired consultant who was counting on his experience but discounted the possibility that having not prepared himself, and being out of practice, he could not come up with specific ideas to bring to this case. "Forewarned is forearmed" goes the saying, and it proves true in most cases because being forewarned allows you to prepare and organize, thus reducing anxiety.

Visualization

Successful people see themselves winning by recalling their last success just before entering the meeting room. Be a winner. Recall your positive scenes and keep them up front for mental boosters. Everyone has had successes, but only the winners concentrate on them, drawing positive mental energy from them. The rest dwell on their fear of failure and therefore do not attend to the task at hand. Consequently, they often fail. They are not able to concentrate on what pays off.

Task-oriented Thinking

Redirect your thoughts from your emotions to what has to be done. This is achieved through the work involved in anticipation. Only by reviewing the material, the homework, and the argument, will you discover the weaknesses and allow for timely correction. Once this is done, the objective reasons for anxiety are removed, and it is easier to feel more confident. Moreover, one can learn to keep talking about the subject rather than dwell on the anxieties it produces. In other words, keep your mind on finding a solution rather than pondering on the complexity of the problem. Solutions come in bits and pieces that must be welcomed and allowed to be put together. Rather than minimizing them, exploit and develop them, and you will integrate them in your context.

Humor

Humor reduces anxiety by producing laughter. It creates a distance between people's points of view, attitudes, and their emotional reactions to them. James Thurber said it better: "Humor is emotional chaos remembered in tranquillity." Think of using it to your advantage.

ATTENTION VERSUS RETENTION PROBLEMS

People tend to blame their memory any chance they get, not taking into account the fact that sometimes there is no memory trace to be recaptured. When attention cannot be sustained the information is often not recorded. William James remarked: "An object once attended to will remain in memory, whereas one inattentively allowed to pass will leave no traces." Remember, seeing is only channeled by looking, as hearing is by listening. We must learn to differentiate attention problems (no traces), from retention problems (traces difficult to access). Only in the latter was there an attempt to consciously record the information, but then it was not efficiently stored, perhaps because the situation did not allow it.

WHEN ATTENTION CANNOT BE SUSTAINED AT ANY AGE

There are a series of situations in which attention is particularly threatened. By anticipating them, we can often prevent forgetfulness, or at least explain it. I have already mentioned a few, but here I have listed them all:

- ◆ when anxious or depressed
- ◆ when rushing
- ◆ when under stress or strong emotions
- ◆ when interferences or digressions occur
- ◆ when ill, with low resistance
- ◆ when tired or drowsy (antihistamines)
- ◆ when under the influence of alcohol, drugs, or caffeine

- when making automatic gestures
- when familiarity prevails
- when you cannot make sense of something

We can postpone doing work that requires concentration when we are sick, drowsy, or emotionally in turmoil. When we are anxious we can expect memory lapses, as is commonly the case with stage fright, examination fear, or the "tip of the tongue phenomenon" when we are put on the spot to remember a name. We just cannot get it back on demand. Sometimes, in a perverse way it comes back in the middle of the night!

If we are constantly interrupted, our attention is diverted. Fortunately we can organize and prevent many interruptions, if only by placing a "Do Not Disturb" sign on our door. When we cannot prevent interruptions, we should put a visual cue to remind us of where we stopped, or we should complete the part of the task we were doing. Efficient people do.

Mind-altering substances have an effect on alertness and judgment. The message does not get recorded properly or often not at all; therefore, beware of excess caffeine or tobacco and stay away from alcohol, marijuana, or hard drugs. They all blur the mind at least temporarily and, in case of addiction, destroy brain cells, leaving permanent memory damage.

Rushing and making automatic gestures are the daily sources of misplaced and forgotten objects—from glasses, to keys and documents that we put "somewhere"—without being aware of accomplishing those gestures because our mind is usually on something else, often on what we are going to do next. Thinking about what we are doing at the time of recording the information is crucial to guarantee a good memory trace. By harnessing your mind you will think ahead and pay more attention to your gestures so that more of them will be consciously recorded.

Because it is impossible to remember something we cannot make sense of, we must try harder to find meaning, spending more time on the subject (which may require new learning, in the case of technical information), or give up trying, if it is not of utmost importance. Or else, we may use our imagination and find a personal meaning to remember foreign words and names of brands or companies, as you will see later on.

The principles of *anticipation* and *pause* solve the problem of most attention deficits, just integrate them into your life and you will feel a renewed sense of control. Efficient people have.

CIRCADIAN RHYTHMS INFLUENCE ATTENTION

Chronobiologists point out that bio-rhythms are at work in the body. There are times when animals and human beings have low energy, and other times when they have high energy. Taking into account these findings will help you choose to perform important tasks at the time your energy level is at its peak. *Biologically, the hours favoring maximum attention for depth of processing are between 9 AM and 1 PM and between 3 PM and 10 PM.* (Notice that Mediterranean cultures live closer to the natural bio-rhythms. Now the siesta has been given a scientific seal of approval!) The seasons also show fluctuations, with February–March being a period both biologically and psychologically difficult, especially for children since it corresponds to the middle of the school year. It would be advisable to plan vacations according to these facts. In France, the school system has, and children take a two-week winter break. Finally, we come to individual rhythms: morning versus evening people. These are tendencies reinforced by lifestyle. Nevertheless, it is something to take into account, even if with a grain of salt.

Another important element is *sleep*. Its restorative effect is well known, and most people should have 7 to 8 hours of sound sleep to feel fully rested the following morning. Studies found that children and adolescents sleeping 8 to 9 hours had the best results at school. Burning the midnight oil is not an efficient way of studying. Too often we sacrifice sleep for lack of self-discipline. Unfortunately it shows in our output. Taking naps at times of low energy helps. Don't hesitate to take a 10- to 20-minute nap, setting your timer to avoid oversleeping.

Studies also have revealed that jet lag affects attention, memory, and even judgment. It is advisable, therefore, to postpone important decisions to another time when the body is not under such additional stress. In most cases it could be arranged.

We have seen how stumbling blocks can be removed by awareness and anticipation of situations in which attention cannot be sustained. Now the way is clear to focus on Attention Management.

PRINCIPLE 3

Relieve fear of forgetting through knowledge about memory and relaxation.

Chapter 4

Memory and Aging:

Coping with Life Changes to Remain on Top

Middle age is when your age starts to show around the middle.

—Bob Hope

A baby boomer writing at Stanford University in Silicon Valley, I can feel the hectic pace young people set. The energy is there, with burnout on the horizon. If we lived in a slower paced world we would not experience middle age as we do in a society where time is money and being under pressure is a way of life. Some individuals are better equipped to deal with stress and the demands of a competitive society, but many feel drained or overwhelmed, because they realize they are getting older. Yet they cannot pinpoint the changes that make them feel less adequate, and they wonder what they could do to keep up with the up-and-coming generation.

An understanding of normal aging combined with a few tips should help get rid of the worries and the feeling of helplessness.

If age starts to show around the middle, memory complaints start to show around the middle years. True, memory function changes with age, and that is no joke! If you are older than 40, you may have noticed more frequent memory lapses such as forgetting the name of a client or the message you were supposed to give him. Although it may be difficult to acknowledge for people who are still functioning in the thick of the rat race, it is a fact that when we hit middle age *spontaneous processes are not so reliable*. That is why it becomes more difficult to record new information and to recall it at will without the help of conscious mental strategies. It seems as if effortless memory were a characteristic of youth.

In middle age one must intervene with a well-planned effort. From now on, it is essential to make it a point to remember. Your new knowledge of memory techniques illustrated in the following chapters will be an asset. But there is a paradox at play: The more you force recall, the more it eludes you. An important psychological strategy to adjust to change is relevant here: *Go with the flow.* Rather than be frustrated, adjust to your mind's new rhythm, and be confident, relying on your ability to learn. Don't let some changes overshadow the permanent qualities of the mind such as intelligence, sensibility, and imagination, which play a big part in the formation of memories. Put your forgetfulness into perspective. Everyone in your age group is in the same boat, groping for words and losing their thread of thoughts now and then, more often than they used to.

Shifts of the Mind

Think of your mind as a sophisticated camera: If the automatic function is failing, just shift to manual, that is to conscious management of your memory, using specific mental strategies that will compensate or offset those changes. If you want to efficiently record new information you must become more aware of what your mind is doing. If it is idling, let it idle but help it focus. This gentle approach will prevent anxiety and its counterproductive obsessive monologues of self deprecation: "How stupid of me not to remember my old friend's name, or the title of the book I just read." Just ignore the incident, don't mention it to anyone and don't keep on talking or thinking about the subject. Although those memory gaps are scary, they are common and a normal part of aging. You will be amazed to see how your mind performs well with TLC. Examples, quotations, and your thread of thought will come back to you before you know it. Thus, relax, the battle for a word may at times be lost, but the war to recover control of your memory will be won.

Look at the big picture. The good news is: *Old* information, this reservoir of knowledge and experience acquired since birth, remains intact in your memory bank. You just need to learn more about accessing it when you need it. Your ability to make evaluations, judgments, associations, and comparisons will always be there to help you. The skills you have developed are real assets that have become reliable conditioned reflexes. You just do it right! Admit that your perception might have been skewed. Rely on these pluses and address the minuses with optimism.

Let us now see what can be done to correct the main changes that affect memory in middle age.

ACCEPTING PHYSIOLOGICAL CHANGES

Slowing Down

It may take a few more seconds to process information while recording or recalling information. This lag in reaction time makes people anxious, which only compounds the problem by delaying recall. As we have seen, anxiety is the number one cause of memory dysfunction. It slams the door of your memory bank. Deal with it immediately by taking a deep breath and using thinking strategies (e.g., to recall a name, first do not advertise your forgetfulness but continue talking about the subject, disregarding the incident). Chances are the name will come to you in time. Let your scanner work at its own rhythm and you will do just fine. For the names you can anticipate you will need, review them several times and just before you go. Using mnemonics such as visualizing an *ant* on the *anthurium* plant to remember its name, will speed up recall and eliminate anxiety. (See following chapters to learn more about prompters to trigger recall.)

Word recall plays a small role in your daily routine, however. Most of your work requires thinking that should not be affected by this change of pace in the brain waves. In fact, you can count on your mind at all times. Realize that you are not at a disadvantage unless you put time pressure on yourself: Your experience will save you time in researching information, finding cases in point, and reaching conclusions—not to mention the practice you have doing this kind of work. Trust your skills and shrug off these minute lags in reaction time, which are scarcely perceived in tasks other than word recall.

Reduced Perception

Eyesight and hearing diminish with age. Partial hearing leads to misunderstandings and slows down meetings. Partial eyesight leads to errors and omissions. Both bring about stress to everyone involved and produce breaks in communication. What happens is, valuable information is not processed into memory. Reduced perception results in misnamed "memory gaps," similar to those of people who doze off or cannot pay attention. In the workplace, acknowledge these deficits and take corrective steps to rectify them.

Reduced Attention

During middle age, it becomes more difficult to focus attention and deal with interferences, interruptions, digressions, and distractions. While distracted, there is a greater risk of "automatic gestures" that do not leave a memory trace, (e.g., putting down a file somewhere, while talking to someone). In particular *"divided attention" diminishes with age*: Doing several things at the same time becomes harder. One has to be more organized. For instance, I noticed recently that I could not shuffle three recipe books simultaneously while cooking as I once did. I realized I had to choose the master recipe and keep only this one open. To my surprise I noticed that it was easy to remember the changes borrowed from the other two books that I had put away. Of course I was using a battery of mental strategies I teach! But it just shows how organization does the trick. I wish I had thought of it before: trusting my memory rather than cluttering my counter with all these books for all these years. Think of your own examples and establish priorities.

Particularly vulnerable are the type A individuals who want to keep going at the same pace, while refusing to delegate. In addition to suffering from memory problems, they are at higher risk of a heart attack.

As mentioned in the previous chapter, *attention deficits are aggravated by stress, pressure, fatigue, drugs that induce drowsiness, worries, sickness, depression, grief, and menopause.* Sometimes it takes time to get through a difficult period, and one should seek help and wait awhile (one cannot speed up grief nor menopause). The intermittent feelings of vagueness and self doubt that come as a result of this attention "fog" will pass in time. You can help to a certain extent no matter what your situation, but you should be kind to yourself whenever you cannot.

The solution to this complex attention problem is rather simple but requires self-discipline: *Get organized and try to do one thing at a time, then focus on that task with all your mental energy.* Protect yourself from interferences with gadgets: ear plugs, DO NOT DISTURB signs on the door, answering machines, alarm clocks. Use your judgment to prioritize, get the rest you need, and learn memory systems. Give yourself plenty of time to avoid feeling rushed. Time seems to speed past us in middle age. Paradoxically you will gain control by taking the time you need to quiet down and think. Get into the habit of taking a break when your mind is not clear. Breathe deeply, take a short walk to the water fountain, stretch your back, change activities if you can, and then come back to your task. You will feel and think better.

Menopause

Nowadays there are more middle age women working out of necessity as well as choice. They worry about how menopausal symptoms will affect their careers. Many complain about mental fuzziness that leaves them fumbling for the name of some common object. Menopause touches women differently. It would be unfair to suggest that women cannot function at this time in their lives. In some cases it may be no worse than PMS, which plagues some women every month of their lives with mood swings and irritability. However, the hormonal changes in menopause affect the ability to concentrate. Sleep interruptions are one of the main causes of mental dysfunction.

Physical and emotional discomfort may be dealt with, and so can the temporary blur of the mind. Once you develop the habit of

Selective Attention (see next chapter), your focus will be there when you need it. *The most important thing is not to advertise your perceived helplessness.* Avoid getting anxious. Mistakes can be corrected. Keep your calm, breathe deeply and *take your time to do your best.* If you do not feel handicapped, you will work around the discomforts with confidence in the mental strategies you already use efficiently. You will also be more open to learning new ones to become more organized, more observant, a better listener, and a better reader. Trusting your mind will restore confidence, and your performance will improve.

Be kind to yourself, and stop comparing your present performance to your earlier ones. Under the circumstances you are not being objective. On one hand your performance may be better than you think, for you may come across much better than you feel. On the other hand, you may truly be burdened by more material than before (e.g., the number of catalogues I have to sort out each day in the mail has increased; on TV, cable has multiplied the options and it is harder to keep track of every item as you preview the program). Too many choices! Someone remarked that computers that were supposed to save time shuffling paper, have failed miserably in this respect: indeed, we print more copies of what we do and often get confused with all these versions. I have learned to throw away the old ones as I go, and keep only two—the last original and the new edited printout.

And finally, look around you, many bright successful women are active at this time of their lives. Although they may have an easier menopause transition than yours (less severe hot flashes, migraines, or mood swings), you will survive these difficult years. If they can do it, so can you. The more complex our world becomes the more we have to organize. *Simplify* has become a golden rule at this time in my life. And one day soon, it will all be over, and we will wake up to welcome the "post-menopausal zest" we all have read about.

It will help to learn about the different treatments available for menopause symptoms: the health section of your library is a good resource. To nurse your mind I would suggest in addition to learning memory techniques, a combination of exercise, good nutrition, vitamin E, Beta carotene, B complex, and a good night's sleep. Do your best and stop worrying.

BECOMING AWARE OF PSYCHOSOCIAL CHANGES

Is your motivation to remember the same? Are you overtaken by your routine? Do you feel a lack of challenge in your present job? Need a change? Do you lack competition or feel threatened by it? Do you fear cuts in staff or finances in your place of work? Do you feel overloaded? Have you achieved your goals? Answer these questions, and you will have a pretty good idea of the recent changes in your life. All these situations affect your motivation and may result in poor memory function. Familiarity, negative attitudes, and low expectations dull attention and interfere with learning. Sometimes it is necessary to see a few improvements before one can start trusting again. A memory problem may trigger the needed change to move on to other pastures.

TAPPING MENTAL FUNCTIONS
NOT ALTERED WITH AGING

If one looks at the different types of memory, one notices that some are not altered by age:

♦ *Recognition memory:* If you have recorded it in the first place, you usually recognize a face or a place, although the memory may be vague and out of context. Multiple choice tests are the easiest kind at any age because they contain the answer.

♦ *Associative memory* works like a pinball machine, one idea triggering another consciously or unconsciously. One type is *involuntary memory*: That is how people remember things from long ago in an effortless manner. You know that ideas come as you think. Thus, trigger those lightbulbs by learning ways to prompt yourself. (See following chapters.)

♦ *Kinesthetic memory* such as swimming, riding a bike, writing, or typing.

♦ *Verbal memory* may increase. The capacity to make judgments remains intact although it may take longer to formulate them.

Your experience remains your strong suit. It is memory on tap.

NOTE: *Although visual memory declines slightly with age, it can be rekindled with visualization training. That is why I mention it here.*

TIPS TO TOP: At this time in your life, taking care of your memory requires taking care of yourself. You may need to modify somewhat your lifestyle. The mind needs more recuperation to work as swiftly as before. There is scientific evidence that the following advice helps:

◆ *Rest* your body and your mind at night with a good eight-hours of *continuous* sleep. Short naps or meditation may also be beneficial.

◆ *Exercise* regularly to oxygenate the brain and gain stamina.

◆ Learn some relaxation and breathing exercises, and practice often.

◆ Take B complex vitamins to combat stress, and vitamin E to enhance your brain metabolism, which starts slowing down with age.

◆ Do not abuse alcohol and drugs, which cause drowsiness. Keep alert.

◆ Avoid excessive caffeine, which may agitate you.

◆ Enjoy a real lunch break!

◆ *Rest your mind*: Take regular breaks, breathe deeply, drink a glass of water, stretch your muscles, and think about something else.

◆ Vary tasks, change subjects if you can.

◆ Be patient with your memory.

◆ *Review* the main points before you make a phone call or a presentation. Review your schedule several times a day with a week at a glance. Review your next day's schedule before going to sleep. These multiple reviews pay off.

◆ *Pace yourself*, do not undertake too much at a time.

◆ *Set priorities.*

◆ *Simplify.*

◆ *Always be prepared.* Beware of overconfidence.

◆ *Improvise* if you have a memory lapse. As Dale Carnegie pointed out, you can always change your script and nobody will notice provided you are interesting.

◆ *Practice memory techniques* to keep sharp.

Finally, RELAX, relying on your experience and trusting your instincts.

Now that you have learned about aging and the way it affects the brain, you can take charge and make the most of what you have. It has been said that we use only 10 percent of our potential anyway, and brain imaging research has shown that one can expand the neurons' connections by mental training with strategies such as the ones in this book. It is not the number of neurons that count, but how you use them. If you lighten up and don't take your memory lapses seriously, you will feel better. You will also do better now that you know there are solutions to memory management in middle age. Just do not take it for granted, but actively help it with the use of memory systems. Let's wise up and live up to the Roman ideal: *Mens sana in corporis sano* (a healthy mind in a healthy body).

PRINCIPLE 4

Do not expect you will remember: Make sure you will.

Part II

Attention Management

Chapter 5

Selective Attention:

Observation Training:
Defining Targets and Zooming In

Reason respects the differences and imagination the similitudes of things.

—P.B. Shelley

Whatever we select to attend to is first perceived by the senses before being processed by the mind. Becoming aware of our senses is essential to control Selective Attention and make a recording in a conscious, more reliable mode. Everyone is familiar with the term *photographic memory,* but there is also auditory, olfactory, tactile, and kinesthetic, or *gesture memory,* at play. All can and should be developed. "True vision is always twofold. It involves emotional comprehension as well as physical perception. Yet how rarely we have either. We generally only glance at an object long enough to tag it with a name," wrote Ron Parmenter. Open up the mine of potential discoveries through sensory awareness.

SENSORY AWARENESS: PASSPORT TO THE MIND

People with powerful "synesthetic memories" use all their senses simultaneously, leaving deep memory traces that can easily be recaptured through involuntary memory: it is like going fishing with five hooks instead of one, increasing fivefold the chance to catch a memory. It makes people more alert, more receptive, and more personally involved in the recording process. All these elements contribute to a long-lasting memory trace coupled with more accessible recall. It also provides more enjoyment and a sense of control.

Looking Versus Seeing

Not only do these people see more, they pause and dwell on what they see. Looking involves voluntary processes whereas seeing is reflexive. Looking is cultural, and can be taught. For instance, the Mediterranean civilizations encourage looking at people, the way they dress and act, hence the institution of the cafe terraces. From this perspective the street is truly a stage. "The real voyage of discovery consists not in seeking new landscapes but in having new eyes," said Marcel Proust, pointing out that just using one's eyes could widen one's horizons.

In all walks of life one can learn to look at specific information or essential detail, thus remembering it in a visual mode. Although 60 percent of the population is "predominantly visual" (as opposed to verbal), few people bother exploiting their natural ability to look carefully. That is why it is hard to get accurate information on directions—people go by places every day seeing them without looking at them. They have difficulty describing in detail familiar surroundings. Only looking leaves a mark in memory, because it is a conscious process involving the whole self, and because it precludes a pause which allows "depth of processing," that is, *selecting, focusing, and analyzing* (to be discussed later in this chapter).

Active Listening

The world seems to be divided into listeners and talkers. That means that half of the people we deal with are not really listening most of the time, and it is reasonable to assume that the listeners get tired of listening and often just pretend to listen. It is easier to say "I forgot!" than be attentive to what is being said. One hears this excuse all the time, but it is not a valid one. Active listening is a must in the workplace because it guarantees understanding. By *asking questions or making comments*, one gets involved and, therefore, listens better. By *summarizing and rephrasing* what has been said, one makes sure it is recorded in the memory of both participants. *Review and discuss information on the spot*—strike while the iron is hot, and you will leave a better memory trace. As the message gets across, then, one can expect something will be done with it.

Failure to listen usually leads to misunderstandings, and is often responsible for mistakes in judgment. One tends to hear what one wants or expects to hear. (The same is true for seeing, which explains the discrepancies in eyewitness testimonies.) Active listening restores the balance of objectivity.

Ponder this Chinese proverb: "To listen well is as powerful a means to influence as to talk well." Indeed, by listening you find out what a person thinks and wants and you will remember it. Moreover you show respect and interest. Listening is caring about the other person who will then be more inclined in your favor.

One must admit that sometimes listening is made difficult by poor hearing or interferences of many kinds, including muddled speaking. Taped messages on answering machines are often garbled and the source of confusion. When giving names and phone numbers, make sure you will be understood: speak clearly and spell out slowly names and numbers. For example: J–o–e M–o–n–t–a–n–a three-five-eight, five-five-five-zero-zero-one-two. Then, repeat the whole name and number before hanging up.

Touching, Smelling, Tasting

In our civilization the senses of touch, smell, and taste are taboo or underdeveloped. Taste buds are rarely activated in a discerning manner, except in gourmet circles such as in the French culture. Consequently, the sense of taste is not exploited for memory. It can add not only to our enjoyment but also to our social skills, useful in all kinds of relationships. Touch and smell are associated with sensuality or "animality," hence, they are discouraged at an early age. The fact is that we are surrounded by smells, textures, flavors, and adding that sensory information to something we want to remember also adds complexity to the depth of processing. We simply remember better a product we perceive from different sensory modes. Practically speaking, awareness of the strong smell of a plastic car interior may warrant a modification from the manufacturer, if it is unpleasant. It may be the reason it does not sell. The same is true of color, shape, packaging, and texture for many products.

A friend of mine declined buying an excellent car because the back seats were uncomfortable, and chose the competition. Customers' complaints reveal that comfort is not always taken into account. If seat designers worked with it in mind, we might have fewer back problems. In my new car for instance the lumbar adjustment pushes in the middle of the back, causing discomfort.

By practicing sensory awareness, a business person can improve quality in the product, making it more functional and appealing. The relationship between price and quality is often determined by details other than durability. It may lead to better research on scents, sounds, fabrics, textures, design, color, and materials.

Observation starts with sharpening the senses. It may be one way of fighting foreign competition. If the California wine industry is winning prizes in France, anything is possible. But compare, for instance, imported Italian fabrics to domestic, and notice how much softer they are, whether wool, linen, or cotton. I would say that this reflects the part played by the sense of touch in Italian culture. Beyond the functional, the sensual and esthetic considerations deserve to be addressed, simply because people will be sensitive to them, once they are given the options. Taste is cultural and can be taught. It is a reflection on the senses.

ANTICIPATION

We have described the situations in which attention cannot be sustained. By anticipating them we can organize around them, or postpone the activity. One can also anticipate people's reactions, and be able to offer solutions. Many situations are predictable. By reminding employees to watch out for them, one prevents forgetfulness. This can easily be done by putting written signs in key places like the door, or by having a tape with pleasant music in the background running at a specific time. For instance, half an hour before the end of the day, employees could be reminded by a tape or a computer to answer these questions:

- Have you followed through with your requests or customers?
- Have you mailed your letters?
- Have you filed all the information?
- Did you return urgent phone calls?
- Did you do most of what you set out to do?

Glance at your checklist. If you did these things, congratulations; if not, wrap up urgent matters, or put them on your desk to attend to first thing in the morning. Think ahead and organize, writing a list of tomorrow's priorities, and then, make sure you do first things first. (Such reminders should be done with tact and humor so that they don't appear to be the harassment of Big Brother. Of course they would not be necessary in the ideal world in which employees would have their own reminders.)

Also, by anticipating difficulties, you can be helpful to your staff and come across as an understanding, efficient boss. We know we will remember things that come across our desk regularly because each occurrence (bill, correspondence, shipment) acts as a constant reminder, whereas we can anticipate having difficulties with unfamiliar things with which we seldom deal. In this case, whether it is the name of a person, a company, a resource, or a place, the information should be filed with special care. Do not hesitate to open files, even one for "rare items" or "miscellaneous." Doing so will prevent you from doing automatic gestures: see yourself filing this document in this particular file, and tell yourself your action was conscious, not reflex.

GENERAL PLANNING

William James noted that "Attention . . . implies withdrawal from some things in order to deal more effectively with others." He who tries to do several things at the same time (polymorphic activity)

cannot concentrate as well as he who is focused on one task. The principle of Selective Attention is essential to memory function. We use it constantly when we remember specific information. For more efficiency, it could be refined, by deciding on what to concentrate. Each of us sees life through a personal screen in the mind. Our culture, our education, and our personality determine what we choose to select. We are seldom aware of this unconscious screening. Adding objective criteria to the subjective ones will make us zoom in on what is important for every task.

At work, Selective Attention is often made easy by assignments and specific things to do. If you do them as they come, you will not forget them. "Procrastination is the thief of time," said Edward Young. People who have an excellent memory lighten its load by mobilizing their organizational skills. They dispatch a lot of potential items to remember by doing them when they think of them, or if it cannot be done, they plant a cue for further recall—from simply putting the express mail on their coat to using a good filing system in order to keep track of all relevant information, such as sources for materials and outlets. Efficient people also use a few bookkeeping tips: file bills on the date they must be paid, and each week review next week's batch. Acting is better than procrastinating, it gets things done while unburdening memory of one more thing to remember.

A good principle of time management is *Organize and execute around priorities, and do it now!* It is also a key to success.

Reviewing is another way to make sure the information does not slip away. Review often the things you have to do, the ideas you want to develop, and you will keep them in mind.

Making associations between items, people, and places proves very effective. Just spend a few minutes visualizing them and make a comment on something you find particularly interesting. As you think of one the others will come back and you will remember them more.

Keep up front what you must not forget. "Out of sight, out of mind" goes the saying. It is simple to keep all kinds of *visual reminders*, placing the object on your desk, on your car seat, in front of the door, wherever you cannot miss it (provided you don't rush past it! By integrating the *pause* in your daily life, you will not).

Lack of confidence in reminders, or overconfidence due to the fact you expect to remember without them, may lead you to dismiss them. The more you have to do, the more you must organize. Please do not think these tips are too simplistic, and beware of what you find easy: you may not spend the necessary time to leave a good memory trace. For example, the name Smith, which is familiar, may slip by you, whereas Katchadurian will not, simply because you will make a special effort to nail it down.

Appointment calendars and personal diaries may contain a great deal of specific useful information. The more you use these, the better.

By avoiding procrastination and using filing, visual, and other reminders, you nurse your memory. Like a turbo engine, it will perform better longer.

DEFINING YOUR TARGETS: PRIORITIES AND ESSENTIALS

First, differentiate: What is important should stand out immediately.

Depending on your line of work you have to focus on different things. But a few targets are common to many businesses:

- What do you wish to accomplish?
- How do you intend to go about it? Or make it happen?
- What are your options?
- Which are the mistakes to avoid?
- Which elements are original and will guarantee your success?
- What does your experience tell you?

Once you have these targets clearly in mind, keep them up front by constant review and assessment. An efficient executive told me he kept a card mentioning his priorities at the corner of his desk, and glanced at it every time he went by. This way, he kept his focus on his goals.

People

According to all the professionals I have interviewed or read about, people should be a main priority. They are the key to your success whether they are your bosses, employees, colleagues, or clients. Because you must deal with people, you should set out to remember much information about them. Names will be treated in a separate chapter. Here I want to point out that the way you relate to them determines what you subconsciously remember about them. Your likes or dislikes may tip the scales of positive or negative associations. You may tend to remember the accomplishments of your favorite employees, ignore or minimize those of the ones you dislike. Not noticing people is just as bad as disliking them, because they don't exist and do not get any attention. Personalizing is a way to remember and be remembered. It pays off dividends in everyday business transactions, because everyone needs to be acknowledged and appreciated. A word of appreciation shows you care.

Trying to be fair in the assessment of people's performance requires an effort of objectivity. Beware of your judgments of "difficult people." Simply because their style ruffles your feathers you may miss their positive qualities. This reminds me of my student years. At one time we had to endure the sarcastic tone of a brilliant professor. Many students were put off and consequently rejected much of what he had to offer, which was considerable in his field. Partly because I decided I could not afford poor grades, partly because I felt sorry for the man whose personal life was in shambles, I chose to disassociate the man from the intellectual message, and I learned a lot from him. In business it is necessary to do that and make the most of a bad situation. Trying to understand the person helps, somewhat.

Not all people handle the stresses in their lives graciously. But above all, by keeping your eyes on your objectives you may recognize difficult people's contribution, often expressed through sharp criticism. Their attitude is more likely to change ever so slightly, if you show interest and respect. That is precisely what happened with my professor who mellowed a little. (Note that one does not need to like people to work with them effectively. As Les Brown said, "The secret of failure is trying to please everybody.")

In regard to memory, it often happens that difficult people "forget" important things, making you even angrier at them. The passive-aggressive attitude will be discouraged by your paying attention to their positive contribution, and these episodes will become history.

If *you* want to be remembered, do special things for people: *send thank you notes* or other signs of appreciation; as telephone companies urge you to do, *call, keep in touch*. When dealing with people, show concern for their problems, and be interested in their opinions. In other words establish a relationship and cultivate it. Whenever the opportunity arises, have a kind word or gesture; it will stand out as a sensitive sign, leaving a memory mark loaded with positive emotion. Dare to be different in your behavior and, if you can, in your manner: an interesting tie, scarf, piece of jewelry may make people remember you. "Vive la difference!"

What stands out stays better in the mind. Make the most of this rule, and watch for what is different.

Topics to Remember About People

You must remember all kinds of professional and personal information about people: accomplishments, contributions to your common field of interest, likes and dislikes, and where and when you met them. To capture this essential information, make sure you *comment* on it at the time of recording. Verbal elaboration combined with visualization leaves the best quality memory trace. Do it consciously, itemizing what you want to remember. Then before meeting that person again, facilitate the recall by flashing back scenes of your previous encounter. It only takes a few seconds of concentration, and it will make you come across as a special person whose memory shows caring.

Among other things, remembering words or jokes people say will make you popular. Humor will make people remember you too. If you find lively examples to illustrate your point, your audience will remember it better because it will have a visual and emotional context.

Wearing something distinctive is also a way to leave an impression. When flashing back in my mind to my latest business interview I see a shy man with a funny tie displaying elephants. My noticing it made me talk to him directly. (It is not necessary to use the tie as a conversation piece.)

An interesting business card also draws attention: use color, special print, and a logo or design. I use the forget-me-not flower printed in blue. Drawing attention is essential to establishing contacts. Think of other ways to do so.

Products

The products that are dealt with on a daily basis are easy to keep in mind, as mentioned earlier, but few people know their products well, with reference to style, color, or availability. Good salespeople do, and they are rare. Perhaps it is because too many people change jobs too often, and in the new job they are inexperienced about the new product. In department stores salespeople have a ready all-purpose answer to "Do you carry . . . ?" "Everything is out," they say, feeling they are off the hook. Remembering information on the product helps sell it. Think of the last time you tried to get some information on a camera, a car, or a plant you were buying. The instructions are often vague or seldom make sense.

It is also necessary to remind the public of the product. *Efficient advertisement is a key to success: it should be direct, explicit, striking, different, emotional, and combine images and sounds.* That is why television is a favorite vehicle for publicity. The field has become very technical and sophisticated, as the perfume "Egoiste" spot illustrates: A palace with all shutters closed is presented with the dramatic music of Prokofiev's *Romeo and Juliet,* and following its tempo, one window is opened and shut by a glamorous woman shouting "Egoiste," another follows, then another. The camera oscillates in tempo from a close-up of one window to the view of the whole building. There is a crescendo of sound and activity as more windows are opened and shut by more beautiful women all shouting "Egoiste" in a haunting chorus. In this example you have all the essential ingredients for recall mentioned above plus the technical versatility and the stroke of imagination. It is just brilliant, fun, and memorable.

OBSERVATION SKILLS

Emerson said, "That which we persist in doing becomes easier, not that the nature of the task has changed, but our ability to do it has increased." Being observant is not a gift, it is a practice that comes naturally when we are interested and motivated in a subject. It can

Figure 3

M.C. Escher "Three Worlds" © 1998 Cordon Art B.V.—Baarn—Holland.
All rights reserved.

be more or less effective depending on *how* we are observing. In a work situation one must focus on important matters. There is always room for improvement on sharpening observation skills. It is handy to have a method.

Observation skills can be trained with almost any material, but I will propose an Escher print (Fig. 3) to demonstrate that even with an uncommon and unfamiliar subject, anyone can remember a considerable amount of detail by following a method of analysis which follows nature: from the emotional to the rational. That is how we respond to any stimulus, whether it is a person, an object, or an idea.

Observation begins with mental curiosity. From being passive, one must become active and raise questions with the intention of finding answers. I propose two general questions:

1. Do I like it or not? (or, Do I find it interesting or not?)

2. What is it that makes me feel or think the way I do?

The answers are there in the picture. It only needs to be thoroughly analyzed. Thinking of categories helps file away information in an organized manner: consider size, subject, mood, color if any, tone, brush stroke, and composition. Then, make a comment or give your opinion. Notice that these steps force one to *select, focus, and analyze*, the key to depth of processing.

You must adapt this model to the things you need to observe: a garment, a design, a product, a document, a car, a mechanism, a prototype. Find your own examples.

Faced with the demonstration print, here is how I would react: "I start answering the two questions by saying that this picture pleases me greatly because of its *mood*: it is both serene and intense, due to its subject and the style and manner in which it is represented. I like the *subject*: nature, fish, water, trees, and leaves. But what makes it especially interesting is Escher's point of view: First his *composition*, using only the reflection of the trees in the water. The effect of surprise draws you onto the water where leaves float like water lilies. Through the leaves a catfish lurks, seemingly as astonished as I. I like this element of surprise! The *drawing* is precise and systematic: from easy-to-identify larger leaves at the bottom front we move to increasingly smaller ones until they appear as specks and lines on the surface of the reflective water at the upper back. The *perspective* is interesting, especially drawn into the bare branches of the trees' reflection. The eye dances from one world to the other. The picture *title* is *Three Worlds*. I interpret these worlds as the trees with fallen scattered leaves, the water, and the fish.

I enjoy the mixture of fantasy and mathematical rigor in Escher's drawing. It is meticulous and detailed in parts, and light and frothy in others. I like to follow the line of the reversed tree trunks into the bottom of the translucent pond. The tiny bare boughs form a circle around the fish, the tail of which is curved, suggesting movement. The white leaves against the gray water and black trees are striking. The fish appears in softer shades of gray with a lovely scale robe and whimsical whiskers matching his surprised stare. The more I look, the more I see, the more I feel happy discovering new dimensions to the work. It is both aesthetically beautiful and intellectually challenging to me. That is why I have chosen it as an example worth observing. What about *your* reaction?

Think of your own scenario for observing anything you set out to remember. It may be an object—engine, gear, or screen—or a procedure. You name it and analyze it in the preceding manner.

Comparing

Comparing is often inevitable if the observation leads to an evaluation. Comparisons should be done thoroughly through categories, and given time to ponder. When comparing we look at *resemblances and differences*. Resemblances stand out through immediate recognition. Making the most of them may come in handy when negotiating with clients. Itemize resemblances in point of view, interests, benefits, strengths, and weaknesses. Review them often when thinking about the deal, and use them to your mutual advantage, creating a win/win situation based on your memory power. Although resemblances are usually spotted first, it is the differences one must spend time analyzing, because they are *new information*. So, in order to learn about a new system, a new language, a new object, one must focus most of the time and energy on differences. That's what helps memory, and pays off ultimately.

There is a natural tendency, however, to want to dwell on the familiar, as the inefficient Spanish-speaking student learning Italian too often does, with the result that he does not learn the differences, and keeps talking Spanish with the illusion of talking Italian. Especially when there are many similarities, one must focus on the differences. When we say, "all these models, contracts, all these people look alike," we are blinded by their similarity to the point of not looking at what differentiates them. A conscious effort to restore the balance plus constant training are required.

A technical example might be of a salesperson selling a personal computer that comes in three models: 100, 200, and 300. Each model has different characteristics. The observant salesperson will quickly learn these characteristics so that they can be pointed out to a potential client according to need. For example, the model 100 is the slowest, the 200 is much faster, and the 300 is fastest. The display on the models 100 and 200 is the same and inferior to the

display on model 300. The disk drive capacity on the 100 is less than that of the 200 and 300, which is the same in both cases. Of course, the prices of the three models reflect these differences. You notice that the crescendo of the numbers matches the complexity and the price of the item. These are the points to focus on and keep in mind in order to make a decision.

Think of your mind as a camera focusing on what interests you, and observing it thoroughly with close-ups. I guarantee you will remember. In addition, you will receive as a bonus the enjoyment of discovering objects of interest and beauty that otherwise would have passed unnoticed.

Commenting

Making a judgment is especially efficient to memory, because it involves the whole person, thoughts, emotions, and background. It puts personalized elements in context and includes both visual and verbal elaboration. It forces you to react and act by saying something. Always end your observation with a personal comment. You will remember it much better.

In order to integrate these principles into your everyday life, train your observation skills every day, comparing *language or ideas* in memos or the newspapers, *patterns* in fabrics, furniture, dishes, or flatware, and of course, in material you work with.

THE TRINITY OF DEPTH OF PROCESSING: SELECT, FOCUS, AND ANALYZE

Whenever you remember something, you have selected, focused, and analyzed specific information. This is easily done when the subject is interesting and when there is an urgency to recall it. While you are analyzing something, you are working on "depth of processing," which guarantees a top-quality memory trace. Good recall depends on the way information is stored for easy access. When you *select, focus, and analyze* you make sure that the next time you see the picture in reality or through visualization you will be drawn back to the same details. Recognition memory is very strong. You will be able to retrieve more by asking questions around the categories in which you chose to file the information at the time of recording. For example, you select a product, focus on its characteristics one at a time, and analyze these thoroughly, zooming in on details as if your mind were a camera. The secret of an exceptional memory lies in the ability to focus intensely and narrowly on a mental picture. George Parker Bidder, called "The Calculating Boy of Devon," explained how he used his photographic memory to memorize numbers: "In mental arithmetic, you begin at the left-hand extremity, and you conclude at the unit, allowing only one fact to be impressed on the mind at one time. You modify that fact every instant as the process goes on, but still, the object is to have one fact only, stored away at one time."

NOTE-TAKING SKILLS

Good notes can refresh your memory. The French say that note-taking is an art because it requires flair and sensibility to select the essential or more interesting elements of a text. It is indeed a highly personal and subjective exercise. Whether you are listening to a lecture or a debate, or reading a lengthy report, you cannot hope to remember every single word or statement. All attempts to do so are doomed, resulting in crowded, unreadable notes that reflect one important fact: the person could not separate the wheat from the chaff. The confusion in the notes reflects that of the mind. To improve your note-taking, here are easy-to-master technical pointers:

- ◆ Be concise (use index cards, preferably, and number the cards).

- ◆ First, write references: date, title, author.

- ◆ Take down all graphics, terms, and sentences written by the lecturer on the board.

- ◆ Highlight titles, the plan, and the key words (use colored pens or different print).

- ◆ Do not crowd. Leave spaces between paragraphs. Write new ideas on a different line. Don't hesitate to use several cards (your notes must be clear and restful to read).

- ◆ Use abbreviations and truncated sentences (verbs can often be omitted).

My personal trick is to note each main idea with an example illustrating it. In addition, jot down in parentheses your reactions and comments as they spring at the moment; that is, an association, or question or exclamation mark. This will make it easy for you to elaborate on your notes. It may also save time to zoom in on points that need clarification. *We remember what stands out and what we relate to because it makes sense to us.* It will undoubtedly leave a better memory trace.

PRINCIPLE 5

Be aware: Select, Focus, and Analyze anything you set out to remember, one thing at a time.

Chapter 6

The Power of Verbalization:

Listening and Talking to Yourself and Others

The hearing ear is always found close to the speaking tongue.

—Emerson

MIND YOUR WORDS!

The power of verbalization is evident in successful teachers, preachers, politicians, salespeople, and managers—all those who need to sell, persuade, and be remembered. The art of rhetoric is rare, but when it reaches its peak it can be awesome, depending on what ideas it brings forward. Think of politicians like Churchill, General de Gaulle, Hitler, Mussolini; preachers like Martin Luther King and Les

Brown; and the articulate people you know. They have a tremendous influence on people because they touch them at an emotional level. Dale Carnegie showed thousands how to master public speaking and use their verbal skills to their advantage, by desensitizing them to fear of criticism while making them aware of their strengths. He was right to put the emphasis on anxiety reduction, for as you become less anxious, words, voice, and memory are liberated!

Successful people present their message in an unforgettable way through diverse strategies: real emotional involvement in the topic, varied tone of voice, pace of delivery and rhythm, concrete examples people can relate to, and a few simple ideas presented in different contexts, always to the point. All this makes it easier for the listener to focus her attention on the topic and grasp the message. In everyday transactions verbalization takes on a more modest form; however, all these strategies can be used to help the listeners' attention and insure a better memory trace.

The goal of verbal communication is to be understood and remembered. In the workplace, it is assumed the message should be important. To make it easy to remember, it must be well-defined, simply stated, and expressed with conviction in a forceful manner. Strong communicators know their field, believe in what they say and want to convince their audience. They force people to listen, using the strategies mentioned above, relying on rational and emotional arguments. Notice that they always begin and end their statement on the key point they want to make. Often they repeat it as a dominant theme with different illustrations. The more often it is heard, the better it is remembered. The frequency of exposure is an important principle followed by advertisers. People need to be constantly reminded of a product or else they forget about it.

On the receiving end, getting verbally involved is a sure way to increase motivation and spur attention, the key ingredients starting the memory process. Talking about something, giving one's opinion, is the natural way to use verbalization and has proven very effective in our research studies: When people are trained to take mental pictures they remember better. But when, in addition, they are asked to comment on the image-associations (e.g., glasses on the table: "I hope they will not be in the way . . ."), they do *much* better. Also, people have more exact recollections of what they themselves said than what others said. So, get into the habit of saying something to yourself on anything you may want to remember. This inner monologue really pays off. Talking aloud adds an auditory print to the memory trace. You may want to use it with discretion for important items when you are alone. (After all, that is how actors learn their lines.)

To remember better what others say, use the *rephrasing* technique: repeat the important statement in a question form to make sure there is no misunderstanding. "Did you say that Lithuanians are interested in trading with Scandinavia?" Then ask for *clarification*: "Which country and products do they have in mind?" This process acts as a review, the statement being made three times instead of one. In addition, the simple fact of raising the issue signals your memory that it is to be dealt with.

Verbal skills stem from listening skills, often an ear for music. Only 40 percent of the population is predominantly verbal, that is, sensitive to sounds, words, puns; but everyone has the potential to improve verbal skills. These are related to reading and listening. Notice that few people are good listeners, partly because they do not realize the power of listening. When one listens carefully, one remembers. It may come in handy to think of gifts for colleagues and associates, but it is most important to keep in mind what makes them tick.

PERSONALIZING

When we speak, we choose our words, and because they are personalized we remember them better. "I told Ginny to watch her step and not get her boss angry." We will probably use the same words when we think back to the statement in question. This remains true in older age when people tend to forget more easily what others say. If we identify a speaker, we are aware of his way of talking. We tend to remember best what we identify with or, on the contrary, what ruffles our feathers in both style and content. To remember more of a speech we must get involved both emotionally and intellectually. As the speaker talks we should react and silently comment: "She is right, sometimes we are our own worst enemies. We do not have to accept being put down. Neither a boss nor a cop will ruin my day." As Eleanor Roosevelt said "No one can make you feel inferior without your consent." Elaborating on what we relate to pays dividends!

It is noteworthy that vocabulary and memory are related: the more specific the word, the more search for nuance or "depth of processing." Contrary to common belief, vocabulary does not diminish with age but often increases if the person continues to read and communicate.

ANALYZING

When observing something, we *select*, *focus*, and *analyze*. We have seen that selecting involves personality, tastes, and emotions. Focusing is zooming in with almost visual concentration. Analyzing requires a method of organization seen in the observation training. Verbal remarks at the time of describing the object of attention are essential. The choice of words also reflects personality, culture, and the degree of interest in detail. The more one has to say, the more time one spends analyzing, which leads naturally to commenting.

COMMENTING

Once you get into the habit of commenting on everything you are interested in or need to remember, you will find it difficult to stop. This practice is addictive and highly rewarding in terms of memories. A comment is by definition personal, because it is a verbalization of the way we react to it. It allows a pause in the flow of the discourse, and often leads to questions and answers. A comment highlights a person's main thought. By listening carefully to people's comments, you can learn a lot about them. By making comments you actively record the statement and your response to it.

MAKING A JUDGMENT

Making a judgment goes a little further than commenting: it implies you have reflected upon something and have come to express an opinion or reach a conclusion. In combination with imagery it proved to be the strongest condition in our research studies. Some people have never been encouraged by their environment to make judgments; consequently, they do not. If this is your case, you must realize that making judgments in the area of your work will allow you to remember more. In some cases it is not necessary to be judgmental aloud or in public. Just make judgments quietly, to yourself.

OPENING CATEGORIES

As you analyze and comment you classify the information into categories, as we have seen in the observation training with Escher's print *Three Worlds*. The more precise words you use, the more categories you open, the better. Find your own work-related examples, and test yourself.

ANTICIPATING

Words are among the most elusive information. Word recall is a common complaint at any age, but especially as people get older. The more verbal the person, the more frustrating the incidents we call "the tip of the tongue" phenomenon.

These incidents can be minimized by anticipating them in general. When you feel that a word does not come, continue talking about your subject, using a paraphrase, a synonym, or, in the case of a name, by digressing around it. The word will probably reappear in a few minutes, and nobody will have noticed. One important thing I learned from Dale Carnegie is that your audience does not know what you are going to say; therefore, it is in your power to change the script at any time you please. Improvisation is a skill you can cultivate as actors do in order to hide their memory slips. It is human to stumble on words; you only need to learn how to handle these situations. As you are more relaxed, you help your mind. Remember that anxiety is a major cause of memory problems.

Drop it as soon as it appears with the following strategies you can learn: *deep breathing*, *visualization*, *task-related thinking*, and the *assurance* that you can continue talking about a subject you know well. Talking around the subject does help recall the term you were looking for because your mind continues thinking in an area filled with cues. It also gives more time to your scanner to search your storage files.

When you need to remember specific terms for a special occasion (speech, seminar, presentation), you can and should rehearse them ahead of time until you are fluent. This is especially useful with foreign languages and foreign words. In the thick of action there is no time to translate a key term. Make sure you are fluent.

PRINCIPLE 6

Make verbal comments and judgments on whatever you set out to remember.

Chapter 7

The Power of Visualization:

Looking and Visually Recording Mental Associations

The real voyage of discovery consists not in seeking new landscapes, but in having new eyes.

—Marcel Proust

Visualizing is recreating a mental picture of something observed or imagined. Everyone visualizes; everyone breathes. It is a natural response to the visual stimuli. But people with extraordinary memories have an uncanny ability to visualize almost everything, including abstract information which they transform into concrete images. They also flash back those images, thus reinforcing them through active rehearsal.

If you train your visual memory, you will be able to do this too, and start feeling the power of visualization, which is applicable to almost anything from people, places, readings, diagrams, tables, and numbers, to words and auditory information. Before television turned people to passive imaging, the radio urged them to imagine the stories read aloud. They used their imagination to visualize the scenes described. You can set out to visualize the world by thinking of your mind as a fine-tuned camera zooming in and out of focus, capturing lines, volumes, shades, and shadows. Imagine that you are looking at the world through the eyes of a movie director. Everything will take on a visual and dynamic dimension that will enhance memories.

Just form a crisp mental picture of what you want to remember, selecting, focusing, and analyzing its elements. Then flash it back to your mind's eye as often as you can. Rehearsing visualization will make the image stay clear for a long, long time. The more you practice, the easier it becomes, and the more you see results. You will literally see where you put things, where places are, how people look through image-association. Visualize your car parked in this direction, facing that building, close to that tree, and add a view of the place from the direction you will be coming. See yourself locking the door, entering the building through that particular entrance, and you will remember. If you add other senses—projecting sound, odor, and touch—your visualization will be enhanced. Your mind can project almost anything, including emotions, which fortify the memory traces. Just do it!

Visualization is even useful for small tasks like editing on the word processor. To remember the portion of the word you keep after deleting part of it, just visualize it, saying the letters to yourself.

You will avoid retyping what is already on the screen. This concerns people who look at their fingers while they type, but it may also help fast touch typists who may get carried away!

Visual skills are related to looking. Sixty percent of the population is predominantly visual, but everyone can improve visual skills by learning how to look carefully.

IMAGE-ASSOCIATION

Although we may be unaware of it, we spontaneously use the principle of image-association every time we remember an object, a person, or a place. When we visualize something in one place we make a compound image associating the object with that place. If we make a point of recording the image consciously, flashing it back is easy. Thus one wonders why so many of us spend so much of our time searching for things. According to a Harvard Business School study, the average executive, whatever his or her age, wastes about 30 minutes a day searching for things on the desk only! The reason no doubt is automatic gestures that bypass consciousness, (e.g., going through the motions of shuffling papers while one's mind is on something else, usually on what is happening next). By focusing on what you are doing *now* you will avoid automatic gestures and their consequences.

Just get into the habit of taking mental pictures of your actions, putting one thing in one place, giving one document to someone, filing another document in a color file at a particular time.

People

Since people are so important in business, make it a point to remember personal information through image-association: where you met them, where they work, what they wear, what they like to eat and drink, their hobbies (imagine them if you don't see them in action). Also visualize the person giving you material, letters, or gifts. You will be able to use this information at a later time, and it will come back easily just thinking about the person in different situations. (You can also use image-association to put a name on a face, as you will learn in Chapter 9.)

Objects, Contracts, Places

The above are easier to visualize than people because they have simpler shapes. It pays off to take mental pictures of objects of interest, papers that one signs, places where one goes, and it takes only a few seconds. Without special request, the mind does not operate as efficiently. Make it a point to visually record the important objects in your work, focusing on the title, and you will see how good you feel about your performance. A real estate agent mentioned how important it was to remember the houses on the market. But there are so many, how does one keep track? By visualizing specific details of each house, and making an association with the client you show it to, you are sure to remember. Of course, this should not exclude keeping the traditional written list of the properties to show, and crossing them off as you go. But combined with verbalization, adding a comment to your image-association of the client in this house reacting in a way you observe carefully, visualization is a powerful long-term tool. As the house is shown again and again, more details may be gathered, and you get the sense you know it well. For maximum efficiency, dwell on the most prominent aspects to identify the property. Pluses and minuses should be kept in mind to help in the decision of which one to show to whom.

While traveling for pleasure, but also for business, it is important to remember places. Use your mind as a camera, instead of counting on snapshots. I remember precisely how batik painting or cloisonné were done because I took mental pictures when I visited the factories during a trip to China. I can imagine engineers, mechanics, architects, and entrepreneurs doing the same with specific equipment they look at and analyze. Adding verbal comments helps link the image-association to a broader context.

Visuals, Diagrams, Charts

The most common visual aid used in business is the letter layout. As Marshall McLuhan pointed out: "The medium is the message." Indeed, the medium remains printed in the mind better than words. In letter writing, you may want to use the simple and direct block style, starting every line on the left side of the page. Keep paragraphs short and to the point. Stick to the principle of one idea per paragraph, one space between paragraphs.

You can use diagrams and charts in almost any work. Draw them carefully, relying on color and space to bring out the essential message. When working on a project or when writing, use diagrams to put your ideas into perspective. Refer to the ones I have in the book and notice how they summarize and highlight the main points.

Here is my version of a diagram I came across by watching an educational program on nutrition in America. It shows in graphic terms the relative importance the different types of food should be given for a healthy diet, now that we know what causes certain cancers and heart disease. Instead of being given equal weight, the four group foods are presented in a pyramid shape, the foundation of which is the one to eat in greatest quantity. Picturing items adds to the visual power of the diagram, and it may be fun to do if you can, with or without a computer.

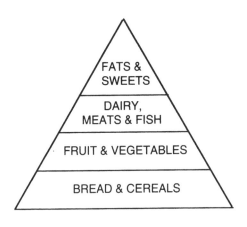

Figure 4
The Four Food Groups

Another example of the power of visualization: *USA Today* is popular not because of its editorial content but because it displays the information visually in a very effective way that is easy to grasp and remember through color charts. To capitalize on the immediacy of the visual impact, refer to visuals and look at them often, flashing back to them in your mind as you think of them. This process of flashing back is what you do when thinking, for instance, about the last television weather report. The jet stream and the falling rain or snow are very striking. The more creative the image, the more we notice, and the better we remember it. The audience may choose a news station for its visuals as much as its anchors.

Topics

By associating topics to people through image-association you will get direct access to the details that count, placing them immediately in their environment. This kind of association requires more imagination than visualizing objects or places, since one must transform abstract ideas into concrete symbols and scenes; but with practice it is possible to do it fast. For instance, you are listening to an interesting symposium on "How to Rescue a Failing Company." Let us say you want to remember the speakers and what they said. As you listen actively, transpose their words into situations, imagining them and their personalities in action, using images as a visual support. First, visualize this assertive executive stripping the decision power of the former management: using fantasy, imagine him forcing them to sign the transfer of power, and their exile. Then, continue the little scenario, illustrating the steps he is recommending to follow. For example, first install your team with the new plan; then consolidate assets; then get rid of albatrosses; then involve the staff in goals; and finally train for behavior modifications. All these ideas must become vivid scenes in the screen of your mind. Imagining dialogue adds to the power of visualization.

PLANTING CUES

Physical cues, or props, are a real bonus, provided they are used sparingly. If your desk is covered with little notes, no particular note stands out; you have gotten used to the mess, and you ignore them all. A good visual cue cannot be missed. It is placed in a prominent place, preferably on top of an object you must handle at the time you want to recall it. For example, a letter to mail on your way home should be placed on your purse or coat, *at the time you think of it*, that is, right after having completed it.

Place paper stickers as emergency signals only, for instance, on your car's steering wheel: "Pick up document before going to work," or "Fill up gas tank now to be ready to go next morning."

Mental cues work just as well once you start using them. You need more self-control, however, to pause and take a few seconds to visualize and think. Mental cues are less reliable when you are under

stress or in a hurry or slightly scattered in temperament. When you go places, you can remember directions or specific buildings by planting a mental visual cue: for instance distorting the top of the Bank of America building by adding a Japanese flag if you are going to meet a Japanese client there. This image will prevent you from having to call your secretary asking why you went there. This, by the way, is from an authentic story of an absent-minded businessman with a lot on his mind.

PLANNING: USING REMINDERS

Order helps memory because it requires organization. When you choose a place for something, you set up the logistics and take a mental picture of your arrangement. You can tell what is on your desk, in each drawer, and you can visualize individual items.

Learning to pause and visualize what you are doing is another way of planning in a visual mode. This behavior helps you keep track of the movement of files and documents that travel around the office changing hands. Just visualize the transaction—the person you give it to—and make a comment on the time and date. You will literally see the difference.

Train your visualization with objects useful to your work, and also to your leisure. You will derive satisfaction and pleasure from it. Find your own examples and follow these suggestions.

ADVERTISING

Publicity responds to the need of stores and companies to remind the public of their products. The most efficient ads are visual, from television spots to billboards to newspapers and magazines (although jingles are very effective, too). Effective ads contain action or the suggestion of action and they also appeal to our emotions. In order to be remembered, they rely on constant review, and they work, provided the focus is on associating product and image. Since millions of dollars are spent on advertising, it is important to point out how to capitalize on the power of visualization combined with verbalization. The most beautiful model in a bathtub will not remind you of a soap unless the latter is clearly displayed simultaneously with the former. Simplistic? Perhaps, but I can see the aloe plant and the aloe Jergens soap with the model and the tub better than many other products.

Humor, emotion, and personal identification also help you to remember. When used creatively, these are pure gold. Think of the Volvo, Saab, Volkswagen, Hanes, and Nabisco television ads. Some of these ads, like the ones for Volkswagen, use a jingle, a mystery word "Fahrvergnugen" explained as the joy of driving, and a funny comment, "Move over Arlene." Music and verbal comments seal the magic of image-association. We all can visualize our favorite ads and sometimes the ones that aggravate us. Awareness of their effect usually determines whether we buy the product or not.

But there is another way publicity gets at the consumer at a subconscious level—subliminal seduction—that will make us choose this shampoo rather than that one whenever we hesitate or have not made up our mind. But one way or the other a good ad is remembered through image-association plus a verbal comment. When it does not work, one or the other is missing. Celebrities may sell a product if they don't detract from it: Angela Lansbury and Bufferin are associated, so are Candice Bergen and Sprint, but the clownish distorted face of "Hey, Vern" is so striking but disconnected from the name of the product, that I forget the product while remembering the actor clearly. The ad may sell the actor but not the product!

The product with its name must be part of the image at all times in order to have a quality image-association. All the creative artistry and technical know-how go to waste if this simple fact is not taken into account. *The powerful ingredients of recall are strong imagery, action, emotion, humor, mood, music, and rhyme.* When all of these are combined, we remember and even enjoy the publicity, as was my case when I saw on the television screen a sail unfolding slowly, a sail made of denim jeans fabric with a discreet but distinctive red Levi's logo appearing on top. Silence, broken only by the squeaking of the sail and the cry of a seagull, holds the suspense while grabbing our attention. A brief comment followed, based on a pun between *sail* and *sale*. Simple, clean, effective. The principle of image-association works wonders provided it is made of clear images. In Part III we will see it applied to many subjects, including faces and names, numbers, lists, foreign languages, and even reading.

PRINCIPLE 7

Take crisp mental pictures of anything you set out to remember, using your mind as a camera.

Part III

Organization Management

Chapter 8

The Principle of Association:

Searching for Logical and Nonlogical Links

All thought is a feat of association.

—Robert Frost

Memory does not operate in a vacuum but is triggered by perceptions, feelings, and thoughts, which combine in a complex web of miscellaneous associations, voluntary and involuntary, logical and nonlogical.

LOGICAL ASSOCIATIONS

Organizing your associations by subject helps recall because you only have to think of the subject category to trigger the associations. In retail sales, for example, one may classify items according to code numbers, color, texture or material, places they are kept, manufacturer, availability, time of delivery, special requests, potential customer's profile, popular or unpopular items, or problems.

In real estate, one may classify clients as well as property in the following categories, which may apply to both: style, size, price range, city or suburb or country, likes and dislikes (e.g., cooking, gardening, sport, hobby), particularities (e.g., smokes cigars, or house with an industrial oven), and time pressure (wants it yesterday).

In any administrative setting, shuffling paper can be filed *mentally* as well as physically as *In* and *Out*, *Urgent*, *Fax*, *Edit*, *Sign*, *Deliver Personally, Make Changes, Review,* or *Messages.*

Notice that the more you elaborate on a subject, the more categories you open. If you do it consciously and make comments it helps even more. Think of categories at the time of recall—they act as prompters.

EXAMPLES OF APPLICATION TO SALES

Associating product to manufacturer or product to customer is of obvious value in daily sales practice. What makes a good salesperson is knowing his or her product and his or her customers.

Knowing the Product

Multiple associations are necessary to remember price, style, make, stock, how to use the product, and other particulars. Using visualization and, specifically, image-association helps. Highlighting differences between similar items whether they are cameras, electrical home appliances, stockings, or fruit also helps. Since there are always new products coming out, there is always more to remember. The need for strategies is greater, and they can be found in this book. The flood of data does not need to be overwhelming. Just taking one item at a time and comparing and recording the new information with multiple references or associations does the job. The busy customer will appreciate the salesperson's knowledge because it will speed up the purchase, and because it has become rare to find competent advice. To help a customer more effectively, listen well to his wishes, rather than give the sales pitch. Once while purchasing a new larger TV, I wanted to know which was the best picture quality in relation to the size of screen and the distance between my couch and the screen. I got no guidance in the matter and ended up buying a 32-inch screen and having to exchange it for a 35-inch screen. Associating knowledge about screen definition, distance to screen, and picture quality would have been the way to help in this matter: For an 8-foot distance the larger screen is OK. Taking into consideration the entertainment center that would house the unit would also have proven useful: The TV had to fill the space. Thinking of multiple associations (from technical comfort to aesthetics) pays off!

Remembering the Customer

Constant job mobility is responsible for lack of interest in learning more about a product. However, a key to success and promotion is directly linked to this knowledge. Another key issue is the ability to know the customer, in general, and the customers who have made previous purchases in the store, in particular. People love to be recognized and they will patronize the stores that give them recognition.

The more interaction, the more associations, the better. Listening and asking questions and making comments will guarantee a good recollection, provided the attempt to remember is consciously made. Showing care and personal interest will make the customer want to come back, as proven by Nordstrom department stores, which specialize in customer service. There, the customer might be even more important than the product, which can always be returned thanks to a foolproof return policy. A shoe salesman told me someone returned a pair of worn shoes six months after purchase and he had to take them back, no questions asked.

From shoe sales to grocery sales, computer sales to car sales, specific numbers, names, procedures, and functions must be remembered. Refer to Chapters 9 through 11 for more specific tips.

NONLOGICAL ASSOCIATIONS

Logic brings about most of our work-related spontaneous associations. When there is a need to remember unrelated topics, however, logic is of no use. That is why mnemonic systems were invented in the ancient world at a time when there were no convenient pencils and papers, recorders, watches, and other gadgets on which we now count to prompt recall and ease our memory.

The concept of nonlogical association is not easy to accept, especially when it is combined with image-association. Some people resist it because it requires making unusual, silly mental pictures, associating items that do not belong together. Once you *think of it as a game* in which you challenge your imagination, however, you stop minding, for nonlogical associations are very effective. Those who use their imagination do better than people who will not abandon their logical way of thinking. We feel comfortable with logical associations like *hand and glove, shoe and sock, glass and pitcher, floor and carpet,* but what about *tree and computer,* or *face and name*? Illustration with what is called in the jargon *paired associates* boosts confidence. Here is a little exercise that will convince you of the power of image-association. Even without the slightest personal motivation, you will manage to remember for a long time pairs of unrelated words, once you connect them together visually. Making a comment reinforces the visual memory trace with a verbal element. Consider it a sealer.

Visualize the following items together, using personal references and physically linking the two, plus making a comment, creating a little story weaving the two together. Spend a few seconds dwelling on your image-associations.

tree and computer	*horse and bed*	*towel and pin*
market and mustache	*oven and moon*	*Paris and chewing gum*
gravel and steak	*sky and shoe*	*manuscript and tar*

Cover the above list and visualize the following single words. They will trigger the ones with which they were paired. In fact you will not be able to see one without the other.

mustache	*tree*	*steak*
bed	*moon*	*sky*
pin	*Paris*	*tar*

Try again tomorrow, in a few days, and in a week, and you will notice that these image-associations are still there! With some reflection you will find many useful applications of this principle of nonlogical associations in the following chapters. Once you are

convinced it works and it is fun, you will also come up with your own ideas to use. For instance, associating project, place, and person; object and price; actor and play; or code and product.

The origin of mnemonics is pragmatic. How else can one associate two things as different as a name and a face, a thing to do or a topic, and the order in which we want to get to it? So-called "peg systems" allow us to visualize things we want to remember on fixed sets of objects. Just visualizing the latter prompts the former, as I will explain in Chapters 9 through 11, illustrating the use of the principle of image-association.

Recall proceeds by associations. The principle behind *mnemonics is using nonlogical associations to plant cues to trigger recall.* There are visual and verbal cues. We will combine both for maximum efficacy.

EXERCISES

Practical Applications of Nonlogical Associations

1. **To remember what you have to do**: When reading your appointment calendar, spend some time linking the unrelated events of the day with nonlogical visual associations. For example: Monday, 10 am: Pick up software; 11 am: Meeting; 12:30: Lunch with Ann; 2 pm: Smog test. Have fun visualizing yourself picking up the software and offering it as a trophy at the meeting and then at lunch telling Ann about your victory, hoping you will be as successful passing your smog test. Using your imagination is the key: Weave short stories associating the miscellaneous events of the day, and you will remember them together so that one will prompt the next.

2. **To remember where and when you met people**, make sure you interact with them, and make comments (personal associations) as you go. For example: "I met Mr. Blois (like the French city) in Carmel Valley. He is a retired Stanford professor with a great sense of humor, and he enjoys his active retirement traveling and getting involved in cultural projects. We met as I was giving a lecture to the community where he chose to live, a lovely place especially in the fall. He had a computer camera and took our picture. I can see him showing me the picture on the camera, and later giving me a print of it, which turned out to be of poor quality . . . and so on." Review these before you go to bed. **Tip:** *A mental review of the day and the people you met helps consolidate the memory traces during your sleep.*

3. **To remember product, person, and place,** try this: "I bought my Lark luggage at the Luggage Center in Mountain View, California. They were having a sale and Marcia the manager recommended it highly, saying even her dog cannot tear at the fabric. The dog sat there unconcerned. I can visualize the scene with all the protagonists."

4. **Search your own practical applications** to the following associative strategies: linking, grouping, making sensory and mood connections. For example, while parking your car, think of visual cues but also smells and sounds surrounding you, and register your mood, the time of day, and the place you are going. You will record a weave of associations instead of a single cue.

PRINCIPLE 8

Make multiple associations linking everything you want to remember.

Chapter 9

Names and Faces:

Associating Name with Face

The name of a man is a numbing blow from which he never recovers.

—Marshall McLuhan

Most people remember names without help of memory systems, but everybody can remember more of them, more easily, for a longer period of time, once these systems are learned. That is what research found out in people of all ages. There are many ways to remember faces and names. The use of name tags is the most common means in the workplace. After noticing the name several times, we associate it with the face. This works for the short-term, but it does not stand the weight of time. We remember the names of our colleagues because we are constantly reminded of them through tags on doors, offices, desks, and mail. Likewise, repeating a customer's name several times during the first minute of interaction may help the salesperson remember that name while the customer is there, but once the customer leaves, the salesperson had better write it down. The reason these techniques do not work wonders is that they are based on *repetition, a short-term strategy*.

Cramming for an exam is another example of short-term strategies: you learn the book for the test, repeating in detail the questions you find most difficult, but you forget them soon after, because you never review them nor encounter them in practice. (A common example is the number of details related to speed or distance in the DMV driving rules booklet.)

To help long-term recall one needs to use strategies that involve depth of processing. Mere repetition does not. Personal motivation and emotion do, which is why we usually remember the names of people we care about. Those of us who are more people oriented have sharpened that skill: Politicians and salespeople show a better than average memory for names, but they also have more motivation and they practice all the time. No matter what strategy is used, in order to make the effort involved in remembering a name, one must want to remember it and do something about it.

In general, people who find names difficult instinctively perceive the reason: they are sounds without meaning. *The concept of meaning is essential to processing information.* Without meaning one must rely on constant exposure to the name, which happens with people or products we deal with on a daily basis. Notice that it is not unusual to hear someone comment on his or her name to allow you to grasp it better: Davies, like Davies Symphony Hall in San Francisco; or Levi, like Levi Strauss; or Mooney, like money and moon. They evoke familiarity to help you remember by association. This is useful for the name, but it does not provide a direct association to the face. The difficulty of remembering the name when you see the face is never dealt with, unless one resorts to a mnemonic system based on *image-association*, and the use of imagination.

Here is a foolproof mnemonic which guarantees recall upon seeing the face, not only immediately but months from now, by planting a visual cue on a facial feature. This requires your selective attention on both faces and names. You will realize that you have never looked at faces and names in this way!

There are three steps to follow in this new approach:

1. Face: Choose a Prominent Feature.
2. Name: Find a Name Transformation (meaning in the name).
3. Image-association: Visualize Prominent Feature (PF) and Name Transformation (NT) together.

Notice that the sequence is important: Make sure you start with the face, for it is the natural way we are introduced to people, and it is the only way to prevent the mistake of projecting a meaning from the name onto the face. For example, starting with the name *Hartley* makes you think of *heart* and suddenly you would think that her face looks like a heart. Of course it does not. It is wishful thinking, and it would not have occurred to you without the name. It is the name that triggered this association. Thus, this strategy of projection cannot help at the time of recalling the name when you just have the face. Rather than trying to match face and name, or look for a logical association between the two, you must artificially link them together with a nonlogical association, here for instance visualizing a *lei of hearts* on the chosen prominent feature.

FACE: LOOK FOR ONE PROMINENT FEATURE

Select, focus, and analyze the feature, describing it in as much detail as you can. This will guarantee that you process it well, preventing you from mixing it up with someone else's feature. Realize you will have many Prominent Features (PF) in your mind if you apply the mnemonic to many people. You want to be able to *differentiate* them well.

Take your pick among *hair, brow, eyes, eyebrows, cheeks, cheekbones, nose, mouth, lips, teeth, jaw, ears, mustache,* and *sideburns.* Do not hesitate to choose striking features under the assumption they may not be there next time you see the face. Most people do not drastically change their appearance, and if you analyze hair thoroughly (for color, texture, volume length, natural wave), you will recognize it in different hairdos.

Here are criteria to help you choose only one Prominent Feature, which is the name of the game.

Look for something striking, unusual, different, or interesting in the feature. That is, choose a feature you are least likely to see on some-

one's face. (Cartoonists and portrait painters or photographers are good at this. With practice you will be, too.) Your impression of a face is subjective, and for your personal needs you do not need a consensus. There is no ideal PF. So, do not agonize about the choice, just pick one and make sure you *select, focus, and analyze.* You will probably not disregard the obvious if it is there. Many times, a prominent feature is not obvious. In that case, one must look at each feature in detail before deciding upon one. Take your time; it does not take that long. With practice, a few seconds will suffice.

NAME: LOOK FOR A MEANING IN THE NAME

For every name, look for a Name Transformation (NT) by asking yourself the questions: "Does the name *mean* anything?" and "Can I *visualize* that meaning?" Many names do not mean anything and you must use your imagination to find one; but many do, and you only need to use that meaning provided it is a visual one (Thompson = Thompson grapes; Moore = a Scottish moor or a Spanish Moor, whichever you can visualize better). Other names trigger an immediate association, like Valdez = the oil spill in Alaska. If not, search for a meaning by modifying the name with an association like Fernandez = furnace/desk. Sometimes we are stuck with the meaning in the name, as we cannot change our names. It is okay for memory purposes although one may not like the association. This applies to names such as Seeman, Gross, Vandal, Belly, and Grimes. Rather than fight it, just go with it!

To find associations stemming from the name, *first listen to the sound of the name.* Disregard the spelling, which sometimes locks you into one meaning and prevents associations from coming to your mind. For example, the spelling of Nichols may not trigger "nickel," but its sound will. If no association comes to mind through oral repetition, look at the name and *divide it into syllables*

(Mitchell = Mitt/schell; Stuart = stew/art; Reagan = ray/gun). If no meaning emerges, *try substituting* consonants that sound very close: p/b, f/v, m/n, t/d, j/g, or substitute other consonants (Moffet = moppet, Ophelia = oval, Nagel = bagel, Xue = suit). This is especially useful for short names, which often prove to be more difficult because there is less material for associations. In this case think of the short name as part of a longer word, such as Allen = Aluminum, Bordy = Board, Borodine = Boarding school.

Knowing foreign languages multiplies the possibilities for Name Transformations. To interpret the images they contain in the right language, one must add a visual cue to remember it. For each language you know, choose a symbol like a gondola for Italian, the Eiffel Tower for French, a bull for Spanish, or lederhosen for German, and so on. If you know German, you will think of Nagel = nail; Weinberg = wine hill. Visualize a wine hill with lederhosen and it will trigger the name in German. If you do not make this connection, you may get Winehill, which may be somebody else's name. Notice that German and English are often close enough to use the English transformation: Baumgartner = tree gardener in German, or boom gardener in English, or Rosenberg = Rose mountain in German, or Rose n' iceburg in English. Choose what you feel more comfortable with.

It is normal at the beginning to experience difficulties searching for Name Transformations. But as Sophocles said: "Who seeks shall find"—truth, trouble, and associations!

IMAGE-ASSOCIATION: VISUALIZE PROMINENT FEATURE AND NAME TRANSFORMATION TOGETHER

This crucial step takes about 15 seconds minimum and should not be rushed. Mentally place the image of the meaning in the name on the Prominent Feature and *make a comment* on the image-association. It is bound to be *nonlogical.* Just play with it. Rarely will you come upon "Miss Piggy" and her Prominent Feature—her piggy nose! Seldom is Mr. Black black like shoe polish. If Mrs. Black has translucent white skin, or shiny white hair, you will notice the contrast and remember it this way. *Do not try to match feature and name.* It does not work 99 percent of the time, and it goes against the key idea of *placing artificially a cue from the name on a prominent feature.*

Provided you visualize the two together and make a comment, the next time you see the face you will zoom in on the Prominent Feature on which you will see, literally built in, the Name Transformation, which is the cue to the name.

The chain of recall can be visualized this way:
> *FACE* → *PROMINENT FEATURE* + *NAME TRANSFORMATION = NAME*

Example: My eyes are my PF—they are large, widely set apart, almond shape, blue-gray, with visible eyelids, and they sit on high cheekbones.

My name: LAPP has, like many other names, several meanings. You want to choose the most visual—"lap" like a child sitting on mother's lap.

My image-association is: EYES ON LAP => LAPP (Notice you can reverse the two when lap on eyes would hide the eyes!)

This system literally plants a cue from the name right on the face.

By *making a comment* you seal the memory trace: "It looks surrealistic, those eyes on a lap!" That is enough to make it unforgettable, especially if you rehearse it now and then while thinking about me. To throw in the first name, find an association and weave it in the context: My first name is Danielle = Daniel and the lion → visualize a lion lapping Daniel's eyes on my lap.

This mnemonic is not intended to work with a list of people's names presented in a line. Sorry, this is only useful for meaningful relations you may want to keep in touch with for longer than one evening. To apply it in a social situation, choose the PF as you talk to the person. Upon leaving, ask for the name and visualize it in red paint against a white wall. Then retire to a place where you can think about a meaning in the name (NT). Make sure your Name Transformation is visual and immediately make an image-association between PF and NT. Don't forget to *comment*. It really pays off! Review it now and then to reinforce the memory trace while it is fresh.

Since it does not cost more to add another visual detail, you may want to visualize a symbol of the work the person does, to replace the face and name in context. Example: Mr. Gray (= the fog), who works at Apple computer (= the logo of the apple minus a bite), has a grooved forehead: Visualize the little apple floating above the fog on his forehead.

Warning: In case you fumble and say "hello Mr. Fog," never try to explain the mnemonic! This will *not* happen if you focus on the name, Mr. Gray, repeating it several times as you visualize its visual symbol. This last step simply bridges the gap between the Name and the Name Transformation.

TIPS ON NAME TRANSFORMATIONS

Since searching for a Name Transformation is the most time-consuming step of the mnemonic, one can prepare in advance. If one has the name, it is easy to find an NT before meeting the person. Take lists of common names and practice, thus having a ready visual symbol for names or parts of names one is likely to encounter. These names can be classified in categories: *names of professions* (Carpenter = the plane he uses; Miller = a mill; Taylor = scissors; Gardner or Garner = a rake; Fisher = a fish), *names of colors* (Brown = brownie; Black = coal; Green = turf, grass; White = snow-white), *names of places* (Stockton = chicken stock; Paris = the Moulin Rouge).

Prefixes and suffixes may be tagged with visual meaning like names ending in *sen, son, sun* = the sun (Swanson = swan in the sun), or names beginning with O' = an egg (O'Neill = kneel in front of an egg), or Mc = Irish shamrock (McKenzie = shamrock on a can with a letter Z), Mac = Scottish tartan kilt, (MacFarlane = tartan kilt with a fur lining). Farfetched? Certainly, but it sticks. Isn't that what you want?

Here the means justifies the end! With one of these strategies, you will soon find a meaning you can visualize.

Once you think of meaning in names you will find one spontaneously, as I did with Covert Bailey, author of *Fit and Fat*. Can you guess? Cover Belly, that fat belly of course, except that he is fit.

Brand and Other Names

Product names can be remembered by the same principle of looking for meaning in the name and making an image-association, visualizing it with the product or the place. For example, *Mikimoto pearls*: visualize Mickey Mouse on a motor bike covered with pearls he is going to give to Minnie. Or, a park called *Butano*: visualize butane gas to keep you warm on the windy and foggy California coast where it is located. Or, a new Subaru dealer is on *Chestnut Street*. Visualize that car stuffed (or full to the brim) with chestnuts. Or, the title of a book on listening to music, *Listen* by Joseph and Vivian Kerman from Berkeley University: Listen = an ear; Kerman = curb/man. Visualize a man with a big ear, listening to a music concert on a Berkeley street curb. Repeat the title and the authors' names as you visualize your image. Stress the sequence curb-man = Kerman. Thinking about *joy* for Joseph and *vivid* for Vivian will bring them in context: just imagine joyous, vivid music. It is okay to tag on verbal associations to the visual one from the last name. As is the case here, abstract meanings like feelings can be visualized in a specific context.

For this mnemonic to work, one needs to have a *visual association as a main support*, so look for one, and I guarantee you will find one in the last name.

USING IMAGE-ASSOCIATION TO REMEMBER NAME AND PLACE

It may be useful to associate a person with a place using the name as a source of association. I once tried to remember the name of a lady who had been especially helpful when I was teaching a memory class. She had sent me a letter of appreciation, and thus, I saw her as a more efficient and caring manager. This kind gesture gave me the motivation to remember her better than other administrators I dealt with. In addition to associating her face and name, I visualized both in a lovely park, which for me characterizes the place where the class was held. Her name, Diana Snow, provided an image of snow falling on the park and on her friendly perky eyes, which I also associated with a mini lake actually there. Then, dwelling on "Diana," I let my imagination go: there she was, impersonating Diana the goddess of the hunt, looking at the ducks with sparks in her eyes—an image-association hard to forget!

BRINGING IT ALL TOGETHER ABOUT A PERSON

We defined what it is one needs to know about people in Chapters 1 and 5. We learned in Chapter 7 how to visualize such information and in this chapter how to associate a name and a face and even a place. But we can go much further, linking together all the information shown in Figure 1, Chapter 1. In addition to associating a name to a prominent feature, we can also connect an image for the person's company, home address, phone number, or whatever is important. This then becomes a package of associations bringing together all the important information about a person.

EXERCISES

Practice this image-association technique with:

1. Pictures of people or authors you read about in newspapers and magazines. Three per day will make you proficient in no time. Think also of making associations that relate to the context or topic that brought them to your attention. For example, I learned on PBS about Isabelle Allende's latest book *Paula*, a biographical story about her daughter's death.

2. New people you meet during the week. Choose three you find interesting.

3. Names of companies or products and their CEOs. Associate the two somehow.

PRINCIPLE 9

Make image-associations between faces and names by looking for a visual meaning in the name.

Chapter 10

Numbers:

Associating Numbers with
Meaningful Symbols

There is safety in numbers . . . or is there?

MNEMONISTS' PET PROJECT:
REMEMBERING NUMBERS

Memory for numbers has been the most entertaining trademark of many mnemonists who have roamed the world throughout the ages, mentally solving complex arithmetical calculations with a computer's speed. Many people still find amazing anyone who does not experience difficulties remembering numbers, and psychologists have tried to understand how people do remember numbers easily.

People who are good at numbers share a unique focus on remembering only numbers. In the eighteenth century, Jedediah Buxton from Derbyshire, England, a number wizard since age 12, seemed to have been obsessed by them. Invited to attend Shakespeare's *Richard III*, he concentrated on counting the number of words spoken by each actor and announced the totals afterward. When dancing with a lady, he spent his time counting the steps taken. This penchant for numbers defies logic and intelligence, hence the syndrome of the "idiot savant," in which a narrow, highly specialized skill of little or no usefulness eclipses every other interest.

BASIC STRATEGIES TO REMEMBER NUMBERS

In everyday life, one notices that people who deal with numbers efficiently are usually interested in them: insurance salespeople, stockbrokers, commodity traders, and baseball fans have that in common. For them, numbers have concrete meaning and they remember them. But for most people, numbers prove to be abstract entities difficult to remember. As soon as they make sense to us, however, numbers cease to be intimidating.

Everyone remembers some numbers sometimes. Need, motivation, and job requirements are powerful enough to make us do *something* to retain them: the time of arrival or departure of a train or plane, the price of an item we want to buy, the sizes of clothing, birthdays of our favorite people, distances in miles, proportions in recipes, to name a few. Most of the numbers need only be retained for a short period of time, and the others are often rehearsed in a job situation as is the case of prices, merchandise codes, timetables, and rates. But the pressure is often such that there seems to be too many to remember! What could make it easier? Any strategy that helps to put the mind in sharp focus can work.

First, do not assume that you will remember, but make sure you will by *making the point to remember*. Say the number to yourself several times in a row.

Second, the simple use of visualization facilitates recall of many short numbers such as addresses, floors, and flight numbers. Just *visualize the number in red on a white wall*. (Or red neon against a black sky if you dislike the idea of graffiti.) Flash it back several times, concentrating on it. On touch-tone phones one can visualize the numbers in sequence like 852 (middle vertical row going up), 123 (first horizontal row from left to right). It seems complicated to formulate in words but it is simple to visualize and integrate through kinesthetic—or gesture—memory.

Third, *make an association* about the number. For instance, your hotel room number may be 707, 737, 747, or 289. Possible comments: "James Bond, small or large planes, nearly 290, or 290 minus 1." Until recently, people did not have difficulty remembering that specific example because they had a numbered key, but with the electronic keys, should they forget their room number, they risk standing in front of the wrong door.

It is interesting to notice that whenever the consequences of forgetting can be a real nuisance, we make sure to remember by making a mental or written note. At airport parking lots, it is mandatory to take cues in order to find the car easily. A mental visual cue is enough if one is returning promptly to the car after accompanying someone. But it is wise to write down the area on the ticket if one is parking for a few days. In both cases it helps to make a comment on the cues: "The car is facing the wall, close to a pillar with a C 20 red mark on it. Red = third floor. I take a good mental picture of the parked car seen from the perspective I will have coming back from the elevator."

In business we encounter many types of numbers: prices, percentages, sales totals, stocks, dates, and times. Cashiers in supermarkets must now remember codes instead of prices, which saves them from having to learn the constant price changes. All these numbers are variable, and must be remembered when changes occur. Keeping accounting books updated is a must, as is making a mental note of the changes using visualization and a verbal comment about the nature of the change. It is easier to remember one general number than many, therefore one should focus on percentages. Example: The new brake parts have increased 20 percent. This allows one to calculate the new price of several items already tagged without having to memorize each separate price.

The competent financial advisor reviews all the pertinent information for a client before the meeting, and can remember precisely the appealing options, keeping track of changes in the stock market during the day. Once this information is communicated, the professional focuses on somebody else's case. This selective attention motivated by the potential sale is very effective. It is followed by accurately keeping a record of the transactions for later referral. The competent lawyer, accountant, or salesperson, does the same. Learning to unburden one's memory is part of training it. Good organizational habits improve it. Keep track of trends, margins, and differences from the norm.

These tips on concentration and visualization suffice for recalling short numbers to be recalled within a relatively short period of time. For long-term recall it is necessary to do more depth of processing, since memory is thinking, and thinking is organizing ideas in a variety of patterns. Provided we have an interest in arithmetic, we can keep a phone number in mind if we analyze it. For instance: 852-32 33. Everyone knows about "chunking," that is, dividing a large number into small easy-to-swallow bites. Analyzing the number in three parts, one notices that 3 and 2 are repeated: 32 and 33 are an easy logical sequence to remember; 52 preceding 32 is 20 more; and 3+2 = 5. If this number sounds easy, it is mainly because it has been analyzed. As the answer to a problem seems obvious once it has been disclosed, so is it with numbers. Try several, and you will see that most are manageable in this manner.

RESORTING TO MNEMONIC SYSTEMS

Many people, however, do not ponder over numbers either because they dread them or because they lack self-confidence and have given up on them and arithmetic, saying: "This is not my cup of tea!" For those people especially, mnemonics are a wonderful addition to their thinking strategies. Mnemonics follow the basic principle of image-association already illustrated in Chapter 9, "Names and Faces."

The best way to efficiently store numbers is to *transform abstract numbers into concrete meaningful symbols with the help of codes or personal associations.*

We have seen that memory systems are ways of remembering information through nonlogical associations. These number mnemonics can be fun and effective. They are based on multiple associations which require using our imagination. There are many visual and verbal codes. My favorite—based on visual analogy and requiring verbal comments to complete the association—is to convert the number into consonants and fill in missing vowels to form meaningful words. It is very versatile and works equally well with short or long numbers.

THE NUMBER-LETTER CODE

0 = z, s (*0* is zero)
1 = t (*1* looks like a *t*: a straight line with a bar)
2 = n (*n* has 2 bars)
3 = m (*m* has 3 bars)
4 = r (*r* is the last letter in "four")
5 = L (*L* is the sign for *50* in Roman characters)
6 = G soft like j, ch, sh (*6* looks like a capital *G*)

7 = K, hard G, q (*K* looks like a vertical bar and a seven reversed)

8 = f, v (in script, *f* has two loops like *8*)

9 = p, b (*9* looks like *p* reversed and *b* upside down)

Let us say a cashier needs to remember a code for merchandise:

134 = Bosc pears. 134 = tmr = timer.

Visualize a timer ticking inside Bosc pears.

Or a lawyer, the number of the law on Civil Commitment:

5150 = ltls = light loss.

Phone numbers are fun to memorize by making a story from the consonants representing the numbers. Thus you will associate a person's phone number with an interesting vignette:

875-4330 = f/vkl-rmmz/s = vocal-ram-miss

567-9921 = lj/chk-bbnt = latch key-baby-nut

Use visualization and make a comment on the associations, keeping them in sequence: "Latch key baby nut plays with a nut and may swallow it." Notice that the emotional involvement in the comment reinforces the memory trace by highlighting the context.

There are other codes as well, like The Phonetic Numeral Code, and The 10-Picture Code. View them as alternatives in case you do not like the number-letter code:

THE PHONETIC NUMERAL CODE

0 = z → zoo		**5** = L → law	
1 = t → tea		**6** = sh → shoe	
2 = n → Noah		**7** = k → key	
3 = m → Mom		**8** = v → V8	
4 = r → rye		**9** = b → bee	

THE 10-PICTURE CODE

0 = disk	**5** = spread hand
1 = spear	**6** = snake
2 = goose	**7** = semaphore
3 = pitchfork	**8** = hourglass
4 = sailboat	**9** = snail

You can also devise your own code by changing the symbols, or you can find meaning in clusters of numbers, as explained in the next paragraph.

FREE PERSONAL ASSOCIATIONS

Since the important principle to apply is finding a concrete meaning in an abstract numeral, one can search for personal associations by asking, "Does this number ring a bell?" Think about historic dates you know: 1492, Columbus discovers America; 1917, World War I; or 1929, The Great Depression. Think about personal data like birthdays, trips, addresses, life events (weddings, promotions, visits), or size of clothing. Think about familiar references with cars, planes, and other machines characterized by numbers. Associate the number to remember to data like this, use visualization and a personal comment, and it will stick. Try it, you will like it!

The more you search, the more personal associations will come to you. I find it rewarding to memorize numbers with my own personal references that no one can guess. It is like a secret code. For instance, my automatic teller machine code is a combination of a gas station name (Phillips 66) and the age of my first love.

No matter which system you choose, you will help your memory by planting effective cues for recall using your imagination and your visualization. Just do it! You will notice the difference. As Woody Allen said, "90 percent of life is showing up."

EXERCISES

1. Train yourself to remember short numbers for short-term recall such as flight numbers, address numbers, or parking areas, with this simple but very effective visualization technique: Just project in your mind's eye the number (e.g., United flight 1245) in red against the sky. Rehearse this image on your way to the airport and you will see how easy it is to keep in mind.

2. Choose a mnemonic system to remember personal numbers such as license plate numbers or social security numbers.

3. Memorize a few important phone numbers with the system of your choice. Use mnemonics, but also make personal free asso-

ciations. Although these require more imagination, they work wonders because they are unique to you.

PRINCIPLE 10

Transform abstract numbers into concrete, meaningful, or personal associations.

Chapter 11

List Learning with the Loci Method:

Remembering Items in a Sequence

It is best to do things systematically, since we are only human, and disorder is our worst enemy.

—Hesiod

"LOST THE BATTLE"

The "Loci Method," or method of locations, is another illustration of the principle of image-association. It was invented by the Greek Simoneides who, being the only survivor of an earthquake in which all the guests at a banquet perished when the roof fell in, was asked for purpose of identification, if he could remember where everyone was sitting around the table. Indeed, he could visualize every guest in his place, and the Loci method and the expression "in the first place" were born.

Later, this method of remembering proved to be widely used in the ancient world, in particular by the roman orators, to remember the topics of their speeches *in order*. It answered the need to memorize in a sequence a series of unrelated topics. Because logic only helps to link related topics, one had to resort to nonlogical associations, using as "pegs" a familiar set of places preordered and prenumbered, upon which items to be remembered could be "hung." This system allows us to store the information momentarily until it is used or written down for further reference. It works as a mental scratch pad and holds information for about 24 hours, so that it can be reused. (In order to last longer it must be rehearsed.)

There are many applications for this method in everyday life as a daily planner, from remembering lists of things to do or errands to run or shopping items, to remembering procedures, recipes, priorities, assets, liabilities, advantages, or disadvantages. Once you understand how the system works, you will adapt it to your personal needs.

Think of it as a game. First you need a board to play on, that is, your own set of places. It must be carefully made of different items easy to identify. *Choose a set of familiar permanent places you already know and can clearly visualize*. I suggest your living room or studio apartment, because there is probably a greater variety of objects there. Fifteen is a good basic number. As you enter the door, go left against the wall, and itemize and number all the furniture and wall decorations. If you have a striking eye-catching rug, name it first; name last what is in the center, such as a table and chairs. This is to preserve the sequence, which is the most important thing in the Loci method. Based on visualization, the order eliminates the need to remember where you go next. For example, here is my Loci list:

1 = Oriental rug

2 = Records and tapes

3 = Stereo

4 = Rust leather armchair

5 = Speaker table

6 = Blue couch

7 = Chinese horizontal scroll*

8 = cloisonné lamp

9 = Green plant

10 = Fireplace

11 = Aquarium sculpture*

12 = Chinese dragon and phoenix vase

13 = Bookcase

14 = TV

15 = Round table and chairs

The asterisk (*) means that the item is just above the preceding one. The eye travels naturally from the object on the floor to the decorative item on the wall.

RULES FOR THE LOCI

First name what stands on the floor, and next what is above.

Make sure the item is distinctive and easy to visualize.

Do not pick two similar items. Notice that I mentioned "5 speaker table" and "8 cloisonné lamp" to avoid the symmetry on each side. (The couch is often flanked by two similar corner tables and lamps.) All places should be visually different, so that you know where you are at any time.

Never zigzag to the center because it breaks the precious sequence, and forces you to remember when you interrupted it, thus defeating the purpose of the system.

Trust your ability to visualize your own house, and do not worry about leaving out certain things. One generally cannot name everything, but the selection is made on the basis of visual interest, size, and preference. Avoid choosing tiny items on a shelf or something you can barely see in a dark corner. It will prove to be a weak place on which to put things to remember. After reviewing your list of places several times you will become familiar with it, since you already know them all. As you visualize the room you will zoom in only on those items you selected for the Loci game.

Demonstration

Let's say I want to remember to do several tasks in order of priority. I will visualize my first item in my first place, my second item in my second place, and so on.

1 = Mail document	on	1 = Oriental rug
2 = Deposit check	on	2 = Records and tapes
3 = Pick up photocopies	on	3 = Stereo

| 4 = Review article | on | 4 = Rust leather armchair |
| 5 = Meet with Peter | on | 5 = Speaker table |

At the time of visualizing the item in the place, I make sure to make a comment on how it fits there. My document in the envelope is lying on my oriental rug, out of place certainly, but I am not surprised about the nonlogical association, rather, I make the most of it when I comment, "I hope no one steps on it and soils it!" This personal comment adds a verbal seal to the visual association of rug and envelope. It does not have to be profound, it just has to be; any comment is better than none. It is an insurance policy against weak imaging, and in combination with imagery, it has proven to be the most powerful strategy in our research studies. One of the reasons for this is that a personal comment involves thinking and feeling. Emotions are powerful enhancers of memories, as we all know by looking back into our past. We remember best what moved us, positively or negatively. We forget easily what leaves us neutral, therefore, when you want to remember something, get actively involved and comment on your association.

Steps to Follow

1. *Visualize the item in the place* (clear image-association).

2. *Make a comment* on how it fits there.

3. *Flash back the image-association* (e.g., document on oriental rug). *Keep it in mind for at least 10 seconds.*

Multiple Applications

You can use the system to memorize interesting information you hear over the radio in the car or during a lecture or conversation, until you can write it down for later reference. For instance, you may hear about procedures or checklists to plant an azalea, to refurbish a piece of furniture, to assemble something, to open an account or a store; or recipes for cooking; or methods for exercise or success! All these, plus *dos and don'ts* mentioned by specialists on different topics can be momentarily remembered by visualizing them in your places. I also use my Loci to remember the news of the day, things people say to me, and of course points I want to make in a presentation.

Lawyers may memorize their arguments with specific references listed in the order they want to present them, (which is the origin of the system). Witnesses also will find it handy to keep in mind the main points of a complex case to prevent being jolted while under cross-examination. You will discover your own applications as you start enjoying your new skill. I keep discovering uses for this wonderful mental scratch pad. It may come in handy to rely on several sets of places if, like me, you become a fan of the method.

EXTRA LOCI SETS

Highlighting Priorities

Use a special set of Loci for priorities or important appointments of the week. Your den, or your kitchen will do. Choose seven places in a sequence for the seven days of the week. For instance, in my kitchen I start at the left, itemizing:

Monday = Counter

Tuesday = Oven

Wednesday = Range

Thursday = Sink

Friday = Microwave

Saturday = Dishwasher

Sunday = Refrigerator

To remember a dentist appointment on Tuesday, I visualize my toothbrush on the oven with a bright number 2 on the door for 2 o'clock.

You could do the same with another room for the times of day if you are busy and have hourly appointments. You may subdivide as you wish. For instance, if I choose the bathroom for a twelve hour day I will pick twelve places, but it may be enough to pick three: 1 = A.M.; 2 = P.M.; 3 = Evening. This may come in handy if you do not have your appointment calendar with you, and at the same time you will train your memory.

Making Your Point

You can resort to your office space as a set of Loci to memorize the messages you may want to convey in many different contexts (meeting, interview, hiring, firing, sales pitch, and argumentation). While planning the encounter, just visualize a symbol for your first point in the first place, a second symbol for your second point in the second place, and so on. It may go something like this: Imagine you're giving a pep talk to a junior tax lawyer in your firm. Here are the points you want to stress in order:

1. The superiority of remembering facts over shuffling through notes
2. That self-confidence brings credibility
3. The positive effect this has over jury and clients
4. That memory systems can be helpful

Find visual symbols for these ideas and visualize them in the Loci you elected in your office. Visualize the first item in the first place, the second item in the second place, and so on. For instance, in my study 1 = file cabinet, 2 = desk, 3 = word processor, 4 = window.

1. = cartoon: a crossed stack of notes under a bubble idea spelling out "facts" sticking out of my file cabinet

2. = your self-confident self, persuading others while standing on the desk

3. = the jury and the clients applauding on the screen of the word processor

4. = elephant connotes memory: elephants popping out of the window

NOTE: The *Visual Number-Letter Code* and *10-Picture Code* learned in Chapter 10 can also be used as a set of places. It is more complicated but may appeal to some types of intellect. I recommend that you try it only after you have practiced the mnemonic with your living room items.

Although the origin of the system emphasizes the sequence in which the items appear, it may not always be justified, as in a supermarket or other miscellaneous list. In this case, what is important to remember is every single item on the list. Getting them all is the goal. In general use, the order may or may not be relevant. With the Loci method however, it proves easier to remember all the items of a list in order. The sequence often proves to be a bonus, saving you time, gas, and money, provided you carefully organize your errands. Setting priorities with the Loci method can also make you more popular in your interactions with people if you learn to say something positive first, and then state the criticism. Keep in mind that people listen better when they are not on the defensive.

EXERCISES

Build your confidence

1. **Practice** the Loci method every day with at least five things to do or tasks to accomplish and five ideas to communicate or keep track of in a sequence.

2. **Prepare** your trips using the Loci method to pack and organize your home and work. For example: 1. Stop newspaper service; 2. Find pet-sitter; 3. Passport; 4. Medication; 5. Walking shoes; 6. Maps; 7. Foreign currency . . .

3. **Remember** recipes, instructions, or important sequences of events, and rehearse them until you can write them down or do not need them any more. It will come in handy when you are giving a presentation or testifying in court. With the Loci in your mind, you cannot be jolted.

PRINCIPLE 11

Make image-associations between items you want to remember and your set of Loci.

Chapter 12

Reading Retention:

Different Texts Call for Different Reading Strategies

Reading furnishes the mind only with materials of knowledge; it is thinking [that] makes what we read ours.

—John Locke

The way you read reflects the way you were taught to read. Do you know whether you learned to read with the syllabic, global, or semi-global method? The syllabic method isolates syllables, chunking the sentence and slowing down the eye and the mind. Subvocalizing is often its unfortunate legacy, although it also favors analytical thinking and promotes good spelling. The global method aims at grasping the idea and stressing synthesis at the expense of analysis. It gave birth to speed reading and its excesses. Spelling suffered from this approach. The semi-global method is a combina-

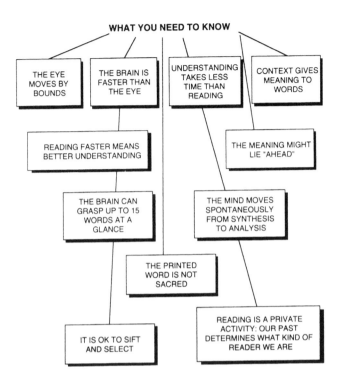

Figure 5
(Translated from Bettina Soulez: Devenir un Lecteur Performant. Dunod, Paris, 1991. Used with permission.)

tion of the two. Featuring the best of both methods, it is the most flexible, and the one used by excellent readers.

The obstacles to your reading potential are numerous. Some are due to lack of information on how reading takes place, others to a lack of self-confidence. All can be overcome, however, through awareness, and understanding. First, study Figures 5 and 6 from the French author Bettina Soulez, a specialist in performance reading.

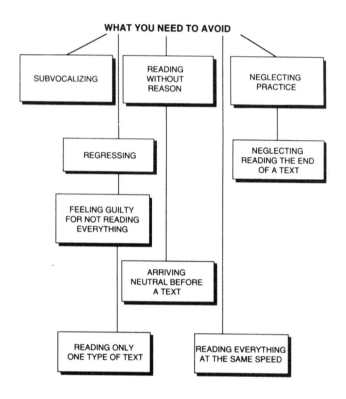

Figure 6
(Translated from Bettina Soulez: Devenir un Lecteur Performant. Dunod, Paris, 1991. Used with permission.)

They reveal "What you need to know" and "What you need to avoid" to become a first-rate reader. Notice how this striking presentation helps comprehension and memorization. Follow each line and notice how all the boxes along a line relate to one another: In Figure 5, the left boxes concern speed and how to achieve it, the middle box is a general remark about how a text should be approached, and the right boxes deal with meaning and understanding. A good diagram summarizes the text and shows visually how ideas interconnect with one another. It leads the reader to visual interpretation in an effortless manner that makes learning and memory easy. I hope that these examples will prompt you to use more visuals in your work. After that, we will look at several reading strategies targeting different types of texts.

From reports and manuscripts to books and memos, one is expected to read in order to gather information that comes to us through these channels. Not all of this information needs to be stored for long term, thus, anyone can learn to read more efficiently to save time and effort. The more you spend time on a particular reading, the more you will remember it, provided you use *thinking strategies*. With a specific goal in mind, it is simple to pinpoint and dwell on the essential. That's what happens when we read for an assignment. Some readers, however, are better than others because they organize what they read differently. The most efficient readers adapt their method to the material. They do not read a novel, a poem, a newspaper, or a report with the same intensity or the same techniques, and consequently, they do not expect to remember what they read for recreation as precisely as what they read for their work. A basic ability to detect and highlight what is important is common to all reading, but certain materials require analysis, reflection, and review, while others do not.

First identify the material, and become aware of what you are getting into. It will force you to define the way in which you are going to read, that is, faster, slower, in more or less detail.

Here are the main reading strategies, and their applications:

1. *Skimming* with speed reading (newspapers, reviews, and searches for specific information).

2. *Reading with imagery* through visualization (poetry, literature, instruction manuals, miscellaneous).

3. *Reading with specific questions in mind: The 5Ws + H* (miscellaneous, for fast targeting of main points).

4. *Zooming in* on the message by identifying the author's plan.

5. *A learning strategy: SQ3R* (for studying and exam preparation).

GENERAL PRINCIPLES OF EFFICIENT READING

The main principle is getting actively involved both intellectually and emotionally. This attitude determines *what you do before, during, and after reading*. Depending on the circumstances, you will spend more time and effort on these three steps.

Before you start reading, identify the type of text by focusing on the title and the subtitles—they highlight the main idea. Notice the length and glance at the structure and the main idea: statement, demonstration, conclusion, results, or findings. Visualizing the layout of the titles, subtitles, and paragraphs trains your visual memory. Flash back to them in your mind as you read, like a mental visual reflection of the printed word.

Active reading implies that you *raise questions and look for answers* in the text after thorough reflection. This is precisely what you do on the occasions when you acknowledge it really matters. You *select, focus, and analyze*, and you remember, not by miracle, but because you have done what it takes to record your information correctly. Make it a point to try to remember what you are about to read. The brain needs precise commands to operate at its maximum. The more focused your goal, the better.

Set aside a time and duration for reading: for example, 20 minutes to read the press review of your enterprise or the business section of a magazine; one hour for a serious reading requiring reflection; and 45 minutes for something you identify as a demanding newspaper like *The Wall Street Journal*. Monitoring your time will help you focus better.

Isolate yourself from noise and interruptions and choose a good level of comfort, taking into account that you need a good back support and plenty of light. This will heighten your concentration.

Define your goal. Ask yourself if for that particular reading you need to grasp the main ideas, examples, or applications? Are you looking for something specific? When and how are you going to use this knowledge?

Choose your reading strategy according to your interest and motivation. They will determine the amount of effort involved. Each strategy has special characteristics you need to know in order to make the most of them. In working situations, for maximum efficacy, one needs to use them all, at different times. Feel free to combine them according to your circumstances.

During reading, focus on your goal and your strategy, taking mental pictures of the key words in the text. Use color liners to highlight them. Most books and documents are not precious.

After reading, review information immediately. Research reveals that in so doing, one remembers 70 percent vs. 30 percent after 24 hours. One can also improve that score, making it almost perfect by sharpening reviewing strategies in order to remember more than the core ideas.

Skimming

Spotting the main idea is often all one needs to do to grasp the meaning of a reading. Only this skeleton outline usually stays in the mind. When Woody Allen was asked, "What is *War and Peace* by

Tolstoy about?" he answered, "Russia." It seems absurd in the context of great literature, but not of memory.

The load of information can be so overwhelming in the workplace that it is essential to learn how to dispose of the useless while attending to the useful. *Speed reading* stresses skimming, pausing only on the important elements you are looking for in the text. This is relatively easy to do if you pinpoint specific information, using the eye-brushing technique, which prevents stops at the end of the words or sentence. It minimizes the number of eye fixations, which slow the reader down. A certain amount of training is required to discipline the eyes to skip the less important words like adverbs, prepositions, articles, and adjectives. Notice that the key words conveying most of the meaning are substantives, nouns and verbs. By focusing on these, one is right on target. To remember, highlight key words and flash them back mentally. Make a comment, review immediately, and review again a few hours later. Reviewing just before going to bed has proven especially efficient—provided one is not too tired—because memory continues processing information during sleep.

In order to get a bird's eye view of the text one must rapidly read the whole text once. The eye-brushing technique forces the reader to keep moving forward in search of meaning. As he does so, he comes to realize that the brain is faster than the eye, for it can anticipate the end of the sentences and paragraphs. The eye can be trained to travel both horizontally and vertically—as is the case in reading newspaper columns—to grasp more and more words at a glance, thus increasing peripheral vision. One important rule in this kind of reading: *never reread a sentence immediately* after having read it, no matter how insecure you feel about your reading comprehension. Look for explanations in the following sentences rather than the previous ones, keeping in mind you can always take a second reading.

At the end, while reviewing the information, it is natural to summarize and dwell on the main points by going back to the text.

Try following these tips after reading a report, an article on your subject, or a memo. (Editors are trained to detect extraneous words, ambiguities, and repetitions, and they work more efficiently if they systematically look for one type at one reading.) The same principle holds true for other inspection tasks.

Learning the principles of speed reading can save you time and energy, your most valuable commodities. Speed reading can build self-confidence by showing that skipping a few words may be a strategy rather than a mistake, another application of Selective Attention. This type of reading is useful in many areas, from research articles and protocols, to bureaucratic jumble and newspapers. It sorts out things, weeds out the text to highlight the essential message. Since reading can be both subjective and objective, keep in mind that the printed word is not sacred but is there to be challenged. It is okay to read only the points of interest or even jump to the end. Many readers feel guilty about doing that.

Skimming can be an end in itself while searching for specific information, or it can be the first step to a closer type of reading. From main idea and synthesis, the mind moves naturally toward analytical thinking. This is true of reading for pleasure as well as for learning; in both cases we dwell on what we consider important, which leads to thinking and depth of processing, integrating new and old information.

Writing down the key words of a text in "red caps" on a card kept on a corner of your desk will allow you to review important points on a regular basis. It stands as a powerful reminder until you integrate these new ideas into your work. A successful eye surgeon said he improved his new practice by following this advice. Every interesting idea or suggestion was thus exposed and reviewed regularly. This technique is widely used in positive thinking strategies. People are given printed cards to place on their walls, desks, or wallets, to constantly remind them of their goal. Some examples for memory training: "You can improve your memory at any age," "Understanding is not enough, practice is the key to all skills," and "Memory is a skill you can master." A successful reading program, Project Read, sprinkled the classroom environment with positive slogans such as "Yes, I Can!"

Reading with Imagery

This method proceeds from the illustration to the idea. If imagery and visualization enhance memory in all other areas, it can do so in reading. Certain material, such as poetry, descriptive literature, diagrams, tables, procedures, and recipes, lends itself better to this method than other material. Once you learn to visualize and transform abstract concepts into concrete images, however, you can visualize almost any text. You will not only visualize the words on the page but the transformed meaning of those words.

Think of your mind as a camera capturing scenes appearing in succession. Pause on the images in the text, and flash back on them in your mind. Think about the meaning they illustrate and comment on it. You will put the emphasis on the essential: the way the message is conveyed. By focusing on the image or the metaphor you detect the originality of the writer. Let's face it, there are no new subjects—everything seems to have already been said—but the ways to express them and weave them into new personal experiences are infinite. This way of reading is ideal for creative writing of all kinds, from advertising to novels and essays. It is fun and rewarding to associate products with words and images. That is, of course, the goal of good advertising.

In a nutshell, as you read, visualize the text, dwelling on the images it contains. Note how they are connected and the order they follow, and finally ponder the ideas they illustrate.

At the end, try to reconstitute the text through its imagery, going from the example to the idea it illustrates. This review is a prerequisite to reflection and commentary, crucial to further recall. For example, one can reconstruct the philosophical theory of the philosopher Descartes' rationalism through the metaphor of the wax. Solid and liquid wax appears as two different substances, when in fact it is one and the same under two different states dependent on temperature. Thus, beware of perception, for it may be misleading. Only reason leads to truth. This complex abstract reasoning is encapsulated in the simple metaphor of the wax.

Since the right metaphor can capture the attention and the imagination of the reader—engraving itself in memory—you could use some in your business writing. For instance, to explain and describe your ideas, find examples and metaphors: "The spine is made of bones separated by jellied discs that work as shock absorbers. The whole structure is held by a complex network of supporting muscles and nerves." People will understand and remember better what you said.

The Five Ws + H

This technique is used in schools of journalism to guarantee that the main questions are answered: *Who did What, Where, When, Why,* and *How.*

Just keep these questions in mind as you read the text, then pause when you find the answers. Adding visualization can enhance this technique by flashing the scene in your mind's eye. You will find that it works well for articles, reviews, and newspaper clips.

Last, but not least, think about the tone of the piece and make a comment. Do you have an opinion on the subject? Do you agree with the author? Why? Spending time on a review monologue is processing the information for long-term recall. This has to be done with any strategy.

Zooming In on the Author's Plan

Here the goal is to spot sign words that reveal the plan used by the author to convey his message. According to Professor Bonnie Meyer, who directed a successful research project on reading retention, there are five possible plans: *description, sequence, problem/ solution, comparison,* and *cause/effect.*

After identifying the author's plan, one summarizes the text with a sentence exposing its structure using the key words. For example, "The cooling of the temperature *is caused* by a mass of polar air pouring down the continent." The key words revealing the cause/effect plan are emphasized. This technique aims at immediately grasping the purpose of the text. It is especially useful for reading advertising or consumers' and general information.

A Learning Strategy: SQ3R

This strategy is a package of several techniques previously discussed, with the exception of "recitation." Incidentally, this step is the one most commonly mentioned at school to help students memorize. The combination of these steps guarantees results, because it involves more time thinking. *Studying is integrating new knowledge with old by thorough and frequent reviews allowing depth of processing.*

◆ <u>S</u>urvey the text to get a general idea of what it is about.

◆ <u>Q</u>uestion by rephrasing the titles into questions, thus embarking upon a quest to find answers.

◆ <u>R</u>ead with urgency, actively looking for main ideas, which are the answers to your questions.

◆ <u>R</u>ecite those main ideas to yourself. Pause and take notes.

◆ <u>R</u>eview immediately, summarizing and commenting with your notes. Make an outline, use diagrams, and look for examples illustrating the ideas. Review them before going to bed, then 12 hours later, then 24 hours later, and keep that going, multiplying the time by two for maximum long-term retention.

Keep in mind that, ultimately, the information only stays alive in your active memory file if you use it. Otherwise, it will naturally shift to a less accessible area. What has been studied in depth leaves powerful traces, however, and can be recaptured when given the opportunity. That is why a solid education is the best investment one can make. It facilitates later learning, which becomes more difficult with age. Considering that in the future most people will have to change jobs at one time or another, it is important to improve reading retention.

GENERAL STRATEGIES TO ENHANCE RECALL

No matter what specific strategy is used while reading, if one wants to remember the information for longer than 24 hours, one must immediately pause and elaborate to store the information on different levels, both intellectual and emotional. This depth of processing is achieved by the following steps:

- ◆ Summarizing and rephrasing key paragraphs or chapters
- ◆ Commenting and making personal associations
- ◆ Evaluating and discussing (alone and with others)
- ◆ Elaborating on the reading (including writing related thoughts on the subject)
- ◆ Reviewing immediately and often (on your own)
- ◆ Communicating the information to someone (reviewing with others)
- ◆ Using the information in different contexts
- ◆ Integrating it in your life and work (constant reminders)

EXERCISES

1. Choose one magazine or newspaper article per day and try to remember its contents by reading actively with one of the above strategies. Make it a point to tell someone about what you read.

2. Read a short story or a poem with the imagery method, visualizing the contents of the text (not the printed page). You will sharpen your visual memory and will remember better.

3. Raise the five Ws + H questions and answer them as you read a text that interests you. Then review them immediately *after* reading. Check your memory the next day.

4. Zoom in on the author's plan to get the main idea fast while reading a newspaper article. Try this strategy daily. You will soon notice that your mind focuses better.

PRINCIPLE 12

Read actively with questions in mind, and review immediately after.

Chapter 13

Foreign Languages:

Success in the Global Economy Requires
Success in Communication Across
Languages

The only living language is the language in which we think and have our being.

—Antonio Machado

For the business person dealing with foreigners, understanding some of their languages and customs is mandatory. From memorizing just a few words to mastering the language, there is only the need for motivation and self-confidence. The carrot may be a trip to a foreign country or the prospect of communicating more effectively with clients or suppliers. Once you think it is possible to learn a foreign language as effectively as you might have learned computer language, you will put the effort into it. With a few pointers, you will benefit from any good teaching method. I hope you will choose one that emphasizes direct communication in the new language and lots of oral practice, leaving translation to a later stage of proficiency. Above all, do not be afraid of making mistakes. Ask for corrections and clarifications. Most people feel flattered you made the effort to learn their language. The difficulty of learning a new language varies from language to language and depends on how it relates to your mother tongue.

Foreign languages are becoming more important now that the world economy is interdependent. They are certainly a must in Europe. In the United States, specifically Florida, Texas, and California, the Hispanic population is increasing so fast that one cannot ignore Spanish anymore. It has crept into eating habits, and everyone knows to what "taco," "enchilada," "tortilla," "fajita," "burrito," and "salsa" refer. The frequent use of these terms in fast-food restaurants makes it easy to remember. The Asians come from varied cultures, each with its own language, and one cannot hope to learn them all. But after frequenting Chinese or Japanese restaurants, one learns many words like "mu shu," "won ton," "sushi," "sashimi," and "yakatori." This proves easy because the words mean something tangible and visible.

A language, however, is more than nouns; it implies abstract concepts like grammar and syntax. The difficulty lies in learning their different frames of reference. The more languages one knows, the easier the next is, especially if it belongs to the same family. There are Latin languages (French, Italian, Spanish, Portuguese), Anglo-Saxon languages (English, German, Dutch), Scandinavian languages (Swedish, Norwegian, Finnish, Danish), Slavic, Arabic languages, and others. Within their family, there are many common denominators that are easy to recognize as old knowledge that need only be recycled in a new context. In this case, learning should focus on the differences between the languages. For example, "mother" is "madre" in Spanish, "mere" or "maman" in French, and "mama" in Italian.

Efficient learning depends on understanding where to put the bulk of the effort. In a foreign language, the new elements to learn are so numerous that the difficulty appears to many to be insurmountable and not worth the time and effort involved. This is true only without a method. As in other areas, using Selective Attention is the key to easy learning. You should focus on comparing and stressing differences with your native language and any others you know that can be of help.

COMPARING AND STRESSING DIFFERENCES

By comparing, we build a bridge between the cultures. It helps to understand what we have in common and what we do not. Comparing is the first strategy one should master because it helps focus on what is important to work on. Resemblances should be quickly identified and easily filed. This old knowledge only needs to be recorded in a new context. Put the emphasis on new learning, that is, on *differences*, which must be learned and practiced at least 10 times in context. They exist in idiomatic expressions, vocabulary, syntax, and grammar.

Idiomatic Expressions

Idiomatic expressions are very interesting to study on two levels: linguistic and cultural. They reveal the way people think and feel. For instance, a French cartoonist made a series of books on the adventures of Asterix, the Frenchman from ancient Gaule. In the volume *Asterix in Brittany,* the differences between the cultures as revealed through language are highlighted in a visual and humorous way. When he visits his cousin, the Englishman says, "Let us shake hands," and he literally shakes his hand with an up and down motion so it sends ripples throughout his body. The Frenchman by contrast "squeezes" his in a firm single movement, saying "Serrons-nous la main." There is a difference in perception and attitude. One other difference to notice is the English plural "hands" versus the singular equivalent in French "la main." You may comment that two hands shake in English while only one squeezes in French.

Vocabulary

Vocabulary reveals differences, including exact spelling. For instance, many words from Latin origin are spelled differently in the diverse languages that have assimilated them: Independence in English, independance in French. Just focus on the vowel *a* or *e* and visualize it as you pronounce it in each language. You can also highlight it in color in your textbook; or using your imagination, you might visualize a capital *A* in the shape of the Eiffel Tower.

Borrowed words can often change meaning. These are referred to as "false friends" because they are misleading. For example, in French *une librairie* means *a bookstore*, not a *library*, which translates to *bibliotheque*; *une lecture* means a reading, not a *lecture,* which translates to *conference*. French for *the traffic* is *la circulation*, not *le trafic*, which refers to *drug or illegal traffic* only. With the spread of English as the international language of communication, anglicisms are creeping into every language, and in the last example, you may hear cosmopolitan French people use the word *trafic* incorrectly by applying the English meaning.

Other examples: *une collection* in French does not translate as *collection* in the context of *money collection*. The idiomatic expression for *to make a collection* is *faire la quete*. The same is true for *garbage collection*, which is *ramassage des ordures*. Only in the arts or hobbies is *collection* the same word in both languages.

Accuracy is very important at all times but especially at the beginning, for mistakes are twice as hard to correct later on. Thank goodness for the availability and use of audio and videotapes. Listen carefully and repeat, recording yourself. Compare and try to mimic the native speaker.

Phonetics

Phonetics, or pronunciation, is often a stumbling block, because people fail to search their own language for similar sounds. From their own language they must analyze the difference with the new sound. This does not require formal knowledge of technical terms or phonetic signs, which can be found in dictionaries, but it calls for observation skills to describe sounds.

Some people are gifted with a musical ear; they have no problem reproducing sounds. Others must work hard and often only reach an approximation. Unless you want to become a specialist, the criteria should be what is good enough for communication. Focus on being understood, not on getting it perfect. A case of how a mispronounced word can cause a stir comes to my mind: When the sexy French actress Brigitte Bardot was asked in an interview in English "What is the most important thing in your life?" she an-

swered with a strong French accent "Happiness!" But alas, her pronunciation, with emphasis on the second syllable, led to another interpretation and the birth of a joke.

To avoid sticky errors, a teacher or a native speaker can give you the assurance you seek. You will profit more from taking a class than by learning all by yourself—and you will have more fun! Reserve the use of tapes for additional study practice.

VERBALIZING, MAKING ASSOCIATIONS AND COMMENTS

By commenting on the differences, one gets personally and emotionally involved. This reinforces the memory trace. Using one's imagination often helps as is the case in remembering a rule exception: French is the only language from Latin origin in which the verb *to hope* is followed by the indicative, the mode of reality, and not the subjunctive, the mode of wishful thinking or unreality. Just imagine the French so sure of themselves that when they say "I hope she comes"—"J'espere qu'elle viendra," (future)—they assume she will. As you notice, the comments may be analytical or anecdotal, serious or humorous. Just make sure you comment on new and difficult items, and you will remember.

Exercises to integrate vocabulary and grammar are a must. By verbalizing the words into context you make them concrete and easier to remember. A simple, effective exercise is to combine six to eight elements together in a short paragraph. Have it corrected by someone competent, and review it several times. For example, imagine a story a foreigner could come up with learning the following words: *toad, pond, bamboo, to stroll, because, at noon, the more the merrier*. Do the same to integrate new vocabulary. This also proves helpful in our mother tongue when we come up with a new term.

For even better results, you can combine verbalization and visualization by forming a mental picture of what you say. This strengthens the memory trace.

Research on language acquisition shows that it must actively be learned *in context*, each item reviewed at least six times before it is integrated. If you give yourself time and opportunity, you will succeed.

Visualizing

Visualization bypasses translation. Get into the habit of thinking and visualizing the meaning in the foreign words, repeating the sounds with correct pronunciation. Imagine the foreign context, for instance, *Se promener,* which means *to stroll.* Visualize yourself strolling down the Champs Elysees in Paris, or any other French street you may have seen in pictures: *Je me promene sur les Champs Elysees*. Notice that the English word *promenade* comes from the same root. Any connection to previous learning will help. Notice that in French the verb is reflexive: it uses "me" for "myself." Say to yourself that the French have a more intense, aware way of strolling. Visualizing idiomatic expressions makes them lively, as was the case in the aforementioned example of Asterix being literally "shaken" by his British cousin. Visualizing spelling in bold red letters against a white wall is very effective. Focus on the difficult part and you will remember even better.

Writing helps visualize. Make sure you write and rewrite new words correctly, especially in context.

REVIEWING REGULARLY

It is normal to have the impression of having forgotten a language never used. Even your mother tongue will withdraw if you never use it. It will have slipped to the gray zone, waiting to be reawakened when the need arises. The rusty feeling one encounters then is normal. One searches for words, the active vocabulary having shrunk considerably, although the passive vocabulary is still there when one understands. Note the two kinds of memory at work. Be kind to your memory, and expose yourself to the language by reading newspapers and magazines and listening to the radio or television. I do that every time I travel, to prepare myself for the language shock. I notice I am fluent more rapidly. As I enter my hotel room, I usually turn on the television or the radio. While I unpack, I am already immersing myself in the sounds of the language.

Only constant review will keep the information up front in your active file. Take this into account, focusing on what is important at the time and using all sorts of cues, visual and auditory in particular, to help you recall what you will need. Notice how practical it is to be able to discard what has been completed. Forgetting is part of normal memory function. It clears the way for the pressing issues. Use the information or expect to lose it, at least temporarily. You will feel better once you know you can recall information when needed, as with languages seldom used.

EXERCISES

Vocabulary strategies:

- Look for extra meanings in new words.
- Use imagery.
- Learn words in context.

1. **Learn new words** by *finding a phonetically similar word in your own language* and making an association. For example, Kirche = church in German. Think of the cherry brandy Kirch and pour

it over the newly sweet smelling church. Or the pearl manufacturer Mikimoto = Mickey Mouse and moto bike. (Learning one word a day or even a week will increase your vocabulary in no time!)

2. **Learn foreign words** by *finding meaning within the word in the foreign language*. For example, I was told that Hitler's real name was Schickelgrabel. I remembered it by finding two approximate words within the name, and associating their meaning in German: schicken = to send, and graben = the graves. I was shocked to notice that his name matched his deeds! A curious but apropos coincidence that will seal the memory.

TIP: Always make a sentence to put the word in context, you will remember it better, and will express yourself in sentences. For more practice you can combine several words and write a paragraph.

3. *Fluency by anticipation*: Prepare yourself for your trip by reading foreign magazines or newspapers, especially in your field if it is a business trip. Start a few weeks before your departure. With cable TV you can also listen to foreign news regularly, which is of considerable help for oral communication.

PRINCIPLE 13

Practice foreign languages with all the principles mentioned, and be able to recall what is temporarily forgotten.

Chapter 14

Strategies to Prompt Recall:

The Ultimate Tricks

In baiting a mousetrap with cheese, always leave room for the mouse.

—Saki

Now it is time to gather the elements mentioned throughout the chapters, to highlight the basic strategies that trigger recall. They have been described in the context of recording and storing the information. Now you will learn how to use them at the time of recall. I have brought your attention to the necessity of practicing planting mental, internal cues rather than relying on external cues only. It is the only way to keep your memory in shape. There are times, however, when you want to use both as the best insurance policy.

EXTERNAL AIDS

Human memory is meant to work with reminders. No business could function without a filing system to keep track of merchandise, transactions, contracts, mail, and customers. The busier you are the more you should use them.

Files, Answering Machines, Appointment Calendars, Business Cards, Personal Diaries

These items guarantee that the information has been recorded and stored properly for easy access when needed. According to the degree of organization, these tools are more or less efficient. But few people know how to maximize them to help their memory. Everything can be sloppy or neat. My mother used to say "It is not more difficult to do things right than to do them wrong, and it usually only takes once." A few tips may increase efficiency. First, be systematic and precise in your way of writing; use spaces and caps. Second, note all the information necessary to reach people. Have a file box in which you store business cards in alphabetical order by related topics (e.g., Jane Jones filed under AARP and Alzheimer). Third, keep track of your successes and failures, and write a short paragraph expressing why you think you had this outcome; that is, what you did right or wrong. Mention others' points of view if you had comments. Later, it may be food for thought. The diary is especially helpful when checking recollection of facts as well as of impressions of past events, or people's roles in a project. Because of normal distortions that occur with time, one may remember things differently than they were.

Charts, Diagrams, Tables

Charts, diagrams, and tables with color codes will direct the mind to the essential in a concrete visual manner, allowing one to grasp the whole picture at a glance. That is the beauty of the saying "A picture is worth a thousand words." Keep them on a board and review them often. It facilitates learning and assimilation in addition to being a wonderful tool for rapid communication in lectures. See for yourself how you will remember better the ideas I formulated in this form throughout the book.

Stickers, Timers, Computer Reminders, Checklists

Some of the external aids to recall are to be used sparingly, otherwise they lose their efficacy. A paper sticker on the telephone, on your computer screen, or on your dashboard is efficient. Many stickers will get lost, or worse, they will become part of the scenery and you will not notice them. *Familiarity dulls attention.* For extremely important matters, use stickers, timers, computer reminders, and checklists *in strategic places* where you cannot miss them. All these reminders have to be planted ahead of time, which implies anticipation and preparation. This is especially true of checklists, which guarantee that every step is done when emotions or distractions may interfere, as is the case at the time of presenting a project or closing a deal. For example, when selling a car, a private party is wise to use a checklist to ensure that everything has been taken care of before and during the transaction. Go over the list with the buyer, as I did:

- ◆ return deposit check
- ◆ smog check
- ◆ ownership transfer slip signed
- ◆ bill of sale (2 copies)
- ◆ warranty (if any)

- keys
- vehicle manual
- service record
- verify buyer's check
- send Department of Motor Vehicles release of liability form
- special tips or recommendations (for nursing the turbo)

To take another personal example, before giving a lecture I check the following list:

- name and affiliation of the person who invited me
- notes on cards with verified statistics and quotations
- technical aids: slides in right order and position, slide projector, extra emergency bulb, extension cord
- books
- business cards

Likewise, a pilot must go through a checklist before takeoff, and so does anyone who wants total control over a delicate operation such as closing up a cabin or a boat for the winter, putting away documents in an organized manner, or simply taking along skiing or fishing gear.

Before any important takeoff in your life use checklists.

INTERNAL AIDS

This book is about urging you to use mental strategies as a way to control your memory—use it or lose it being the motto you want to keep in mind. Now that you know what pays off to remember, just do it!

Pause, Relax, Look, and Think

Before jumping to a conclusion or into a car to go somewhere, *become aware*. A stain on a raincoat may not need to be taken to the cleaners. That's what I realized when I was asked about the fabric. As I checked, I read "*Do not dry clean.*" I could have saved myself a trip and cleaned the spot earlier if only I had paused to read the label rather than assume the answer. This example illustrates how important it is to ask questions and look for answers in an organized way: look first, then think about strategy. Here the obvious assumption proved wrong, and I nearly damaged the garment.

Rather than be upset or panic because you cannot immediately remember a reference, a name, or an important idea, *pause, relax, look,* and *think*. Keep in mind that memory is mostly thinking strategies; give yourself time to think! It is the only way you can mobilize your new knowledge to help recall, the most difficult step of all. If you feel in a flurry, take a deep breath, following Chapter 3, "The Waves," and you are ready to focus. If you have followed my suggestions at the time of recording, you can be sure there is a memory trace stored in your brain waiting to be recaptured. To prompt recall, appeal to your senses to pick up cues around you: look, listen, smell, feel, and taste. Next, use one or several of the following thinking strategies: *free associate, name categories, play the guessing game,* and *visualize*. It does not have to be in that order. You can follow your instinct or preference.

Here's an illustration of how one of these strategies works. To discover the power of *naming categories*, try this exercise. Write down as many names of birds as you can think of. Then classify them in categories and notice that you will think of others within the category you named. For example, "penguin" will open the door to birds in the snow, "parrot," to tropical birds or pets, "chicken" to eating birds, "eagle" to birds of prey, endangered species, and so

on. The fact is that one can remember more names of anything if one thinks of categories. (Psychologist Kenneth Higbee reported 65 percent recall with categories versus 19 percent without, on lists of words.)

To demonstrate how to go about it, let us use all these strategies to remember an important section in this book: *the situations in which attention cannot be sustained.*

Free Associate

Here is a typical inner monologue that could be taking place in your mind: When is it difficult to sustain attention? Personal examples such as interruptions usually pop to mind first. Write it down and think of specific interruptions, such as the telephone, someone at the door, and noise. Now, ask yourself what kind of interruptions are there. Two kinds come to mind: exterior ones, caused by people or happenings; and interior ones caused by distractions, extraneous thoughts, day-dreaming, and digressions. Think about when these occur: when one gets absorbed or carried away. These are emotional states, when pre-occupied, self-absorbed, grieving, extremely happy or unhappy, when tired, sick, or drowsy. Notice how one example leads to the other. Just starting does the trick, and the snowball effect of associations follows. But if you want to remember more, name categories.

Name Categories

Everything can be classified in categories. In the previous example we have already covered interruptions by people, things, personal thoughts, emotions, and sickness. The last example, *drowsiness*, opens a new category: causes of drowsiness. Causes might be drugs or sleep disorders. Think of other possible categories linked to the subject. *Attention* relates to people and the way they act toward others, tasks, or things. The answers "consciously or not," "with or without focus" are categories that should trigger "*no automatic gestures*, and *doing several things at the same time*." By asking why one does such things, answers like one is "*in a hurry, under stress, pressured,* or *anxious*" are generated. Here nearly all the situations in which memory cannot be sustained have been recaptured by using free associations and files of categories. The last resort to get at a few more will be the guessing game.

Play the Guessing Game

The guessing game uses recognition as a springboard by raising questions that may contain cues to recall. The inner monologue continues asking questions and answering them: Could it be some-thing we do or do not do? Could it be related to habits? Poor at-tention habits are notorious. Could habit itself be the culprit? Yes, when we perform habitual gestures we do not consciously think about what we are doing, and we fall back on *automatic gestures*. (Bingo!) *When habit prevails* (Bingo again!) is another potential dangerous situation. Could it be lack of motivation or interest? Certainly, but when do these occur? Often when we do not relate to the message or *when we cannot make sense of it*. That's it, we hit upon the last one. Playing the guessing game produces answers in a domino effect of associations.

Another way of guessing is by consciously being more receptive, keeping all channels open to sensory awareness—look, listen, smell, touch, and taste—and watch what happens. Sometimes it only takes letting your eye travel from one area to the other to find a cue for what you want to remember. It is the case when you are search-ing for a file in a cabinet, or a book or supermarket item on crowded shelves. Just going to the dairy section will trigger recall of what you need, provided you give yourself the chance to look, and avoid letting your eyes sweep and jump around uncontrolled. The difficulty here is that being overwhelmed by so many products, one does not focus systematically on each shelf to pause and identify items. If you do, you remember effortlessly. The cue is there for you to see. Find your own applications at work or at play.

Visualize

As you are actively involved in recalling the information, you can speed up the process by highlighting each step with visualization of precise examples and situations. For instance, to remember what you were doing before an interruption, visualize that particular in-terruption, such as the telephone, your cat, or a friend visiting.

Retrace the scene and chances are you will recapture the missing link to what you were doing then. Similarly, to remember what you were saying or wanted to say when a digression occurred, focus on the digression, visualizing the content of your thoughts and their context.

To remember where you may have left your gloves, your umbrella, or a document, visualize yourself in the situation and place you were (in a hurry, stressed, drowsy, tired, unhappy or elated, depressed; in a taxi, cafe, or at work). Through visualization you will relive those situations, and a stream of associations will follow, bringing back memories.

Visualizing visual material seems evident. Still, perhaps because it is so obvious, it is rarely *consciously* done: apply this to reading material, charts, numbers, locations, people, or objects, as suggested in the individual chapters.

Now, think of your personal specific needs. Visualization works for almost any subject. Try it immediately with your own material, or for instance, to recall the relaxation exercises in this book. More generally, use your imagination to re-create important moments of your life, for as Martial, a poet of ancient Rome, said "To be able to enjoy one's past life is to live twice."

Recapture Mood

Last but not least, think of the mood you were in when you recorded information on the subject. By recapturing that mood you will recapture memories, according to the "Matching of Moods" theory studied by Professor Gordon Bower at Stanford University. In the battle against forgetfulness do not hesitate to use every trick in the book.

The general tactic highlighted in this chapter is to ask questions from any idea or thing connected to your subject and let associations lead you to the next question until you reach what you want to remember. Realize that there is always something you remember to start the guessing game that you can exploit to the hilt by thinking and questioning through *free associations, categories, visualization,* and *mood.* According to the circumstance—its urgency or complexity—rely on both external and internal aids. You will have taken care of your potential memory problems.

EXERCISE

Use memory strategies in the following situations:

- every morning for planning daily activities
- before meetings, especially before a presentation
- during meetings with clients, bankers, retailers, and suppliers
- when planning, setting goals, and defining strategies

PRINCIPLE 14

To prompt recall, use a battery of strategies.

Conclusion

◆

MEMORY AND SUCCESS: THE PASSAGE TO ACTION

This book has outlined a method for controlling your memory at work and at play, since the principles of memory training do generalize. It is up to you to find multiple applications, now that you have become more aware. From passive, you are ready to turn active, and participate in the memory process, both at the time of recording and recall. Knowing what to do to help your memory, you should not feel helpless anymore! The result of your new confidence is memory power, which guarantees success.

You may now agree with the somewhat harsh statement of a successful businessman: "I find 'I forgot' to be an irresponsible answer for a professional businessman to give. A professional does not forget." At least, not if the person cares about the job! Indeed, forgetting can be prevented. Now you know how: through Attention and Organization Management and the use of miscellaneous strategies to prompt recall.

In your daily life, keep in mind the principles of good retention highlighted at the end of each chapter, and apply the strategies. With daily practice you will soon have assimilated them. Understanding, however, is not enough. It is the passage to action that counts.

- Be actively involved in the memory process: it is the key to motivation and control.

- Define and state clearly what needs to be remembered.

- Do not assume you will remember, make sure you will. Prevention forces you to anticipate: forewarned is forearmed.

- Fight procrastination with action: do it now!

- Pause and organize, using your senses and your emotions as well as your imagination and intellect.

- Drop anxiety through awareness and relaxation exercises.

- Use mnemonics and visual tricks to prompt recall.

- Think of associations: compare and evaluate, stressing differences.

- Make personal comments.

- Review information often: use it or lose it temporarily.

- Do not expect memories to happen; make them happen by asking questions and naming categories at the time of recall.

- Do not believe others will remember; make sure they will through reminders and a work structure stressing responsibility, review, and follow through at the end of each task and day.

It does not pay to forget, whereas it pays to remember. By *selecting*, *focusing*, and *analyzing* intelligently what is important, anyone can remember at any age.

Finally, you must admit that a good memory is mandatory to perform tasks efficiently, and to make sound judgments and swift decisions. As Adlai Stevenson said, "We can chart our future clearly and wisely only when we know the path which has led to the present." Thus, to plan ahead remember past experiences, and use your memory skillfully.

Additional Readings

For additional information on this topic, please refer to the following resources.

Baddeley, Alan D. *Your Memory: A User's Guide*. New York: Macmillan, 1982.

Covey, Steven. *The Seven Habits of Highly Effective People*. New York: Simon and Schuster, 1990.

Hancock, Jonathan. *Memory Power*. Hauppauge, NY: Barron's Educational Series, Inc., 1997.

Herrmann, Douglas J. *Super Memory*. Emmaus, PA: Rodale Press, 1991.

Higbee, Kenneth. *Your Memory: How It Works & How to Improve It*, Second Ed. New York: Marlowe & Co., 1996.

Lapp, Danielle. *Don't Forget! Easy Exercises for a Better Memory*. Reading, MA: Addison-Wesley, 1995.

Lieury, Alain. *Mnemonic Processes*. Brussels, Belgium: Pierre Mardaga, Editeur, 1980 (in French only).

Loftus, Elizabeth. *Memory*. Reading, MA: Addison-Wesley, 1980.

Osborn, Alex F. *Applied Imagination*. New York: Scribner and Sons, 1964.

Peters, Thomas J. and Robert H. Waterman. *In Search of Excellence*. New York: Harper and Row, 1982.

Soulez, Bettina. *Devenir un Lecteur Performant*. Paris: Dunod, 1991 (in French only).

Young, Morris N. and Walter B. Gibson. *How to Develop an Exceptional Memory*. North Hollywood, California: Wilshire, 1983.

Index